# Tonight they'll kill a Catholic

# Tonight they'll kill a Catholic

R. Douglas Wead

Creation House
Carol Stream, Illinois

Printed in the United States of America.
Published by Creation House, 499 Gundersen Drive,
Carol Stream, Illinois 60187.

First Printing—March 1974
Second Printing—April 1975

*New Leaf Library Edition*
First Printing—June 1976

In Canada: Beacon Distributing Ltd.,
104 Consumers Drive, Whitby, Ontario L1N 5T3

International Standard Book Number 0-88419-073-0
Library of Congress Catalog Card Number 73-92021

ISBN 0-88419-008-0

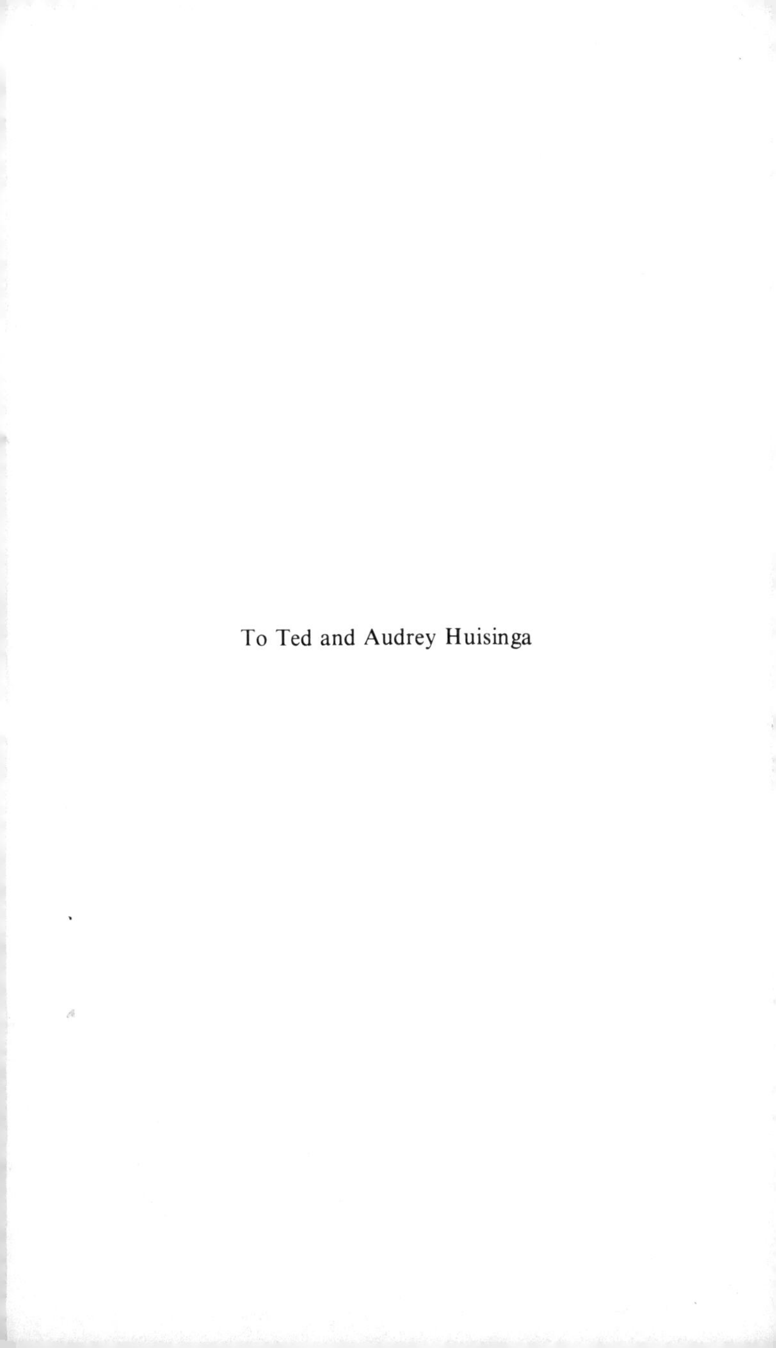

To Ted and Audrey Huisinga

# Contents

Dear Gloria,

I am sitting in the airport lounge in Belfast. It will feel good to leave this place. Last night a seventeen-year-old Protestant boy was shot near Shankill Road, so tonight they'll kill a Catholic. This violence is never going to end.

You know what I am going to do? I am going to write that book we've been talking about. I am going to expose this whole ugly mess. It won't be a long, boring history that no one will read. I am going to organize a team to help me research. Then we are going right into the Falls Road area. We will tour the Catholic ghettos and turn on our tape recorders. We will interview the Protestant leaders. We will visit a British barracks and let the soldiers talk.

This is going to be more than a story of murder and violence. This is going to be story of love, the strongest kind of love—the kind that has endured eight centuries of bitterness and division. I am going to write about Frank and Cecil and Elizabeth and all the beautiful Catholics and Protestants we met last summer. They are the real heroes of this struggle. Maybe when other people read their stories, they will see that love is stronger than hate.

Doug

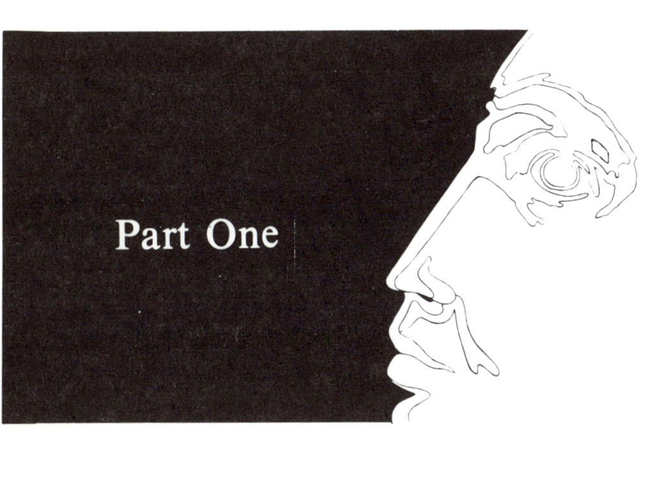

# Part One

# 1

# A Visit to Duggan's Tavern

The Europa Hotel porter said I would have to wait a long time for a taxicab driver willing to go into the Falls Road area. He was right. The one who finally picked me up was supposed to have been brave. As we reached the militant Catholic ghetto, he pulled over to the side of the road.

"I've only been in there once," he said, pulling out a little map. He was obviously lost, but that wasn't what bothered me the most. He was also very nervous. His hands were shaking so badly that he could hardly read his map.

Some little children came rushing around a corner throwing stones and bottles at the yellow intruder. My driver panicked and sped away. I felt like taking the wheel myself.

"Look! I'm on official business. People in there are expecting me. Nothing is going to happen to you."

My confidence helped calm him. He tried again. winding carefully through the narrow streets until at last he saw Ton Street.

I stepped out onto the curb. He was off like a shot. Ton Street is typical of the area. No one in sight—just rows and rows of stone houses. No yards, no grass; just a sidewalk. The street is as narrow as an alley in an American city. I knocked on the door and introduced myself.

"Liam isn't here," a woman said, eyeing me suspiciously. She was an attractive, middle-aged woman, and I knew she didn't believe my story.

"I saw him yesterday in Dublin," I said. "He was supposed to have met me at two-thirty." The more I spoke, the more she began to realize that I knew too many details to be lying. She relaxed, and we talked for a while.

"Well, if you want the story of Catholic injustice, there is a tavern around the corner. Someone's always there." I left 14 Ton Street disappointed and nervous.

"Tell them Kitty O'Kane sent you," she yelled after me.

Walking through the Falls Road area for the first time was an eerie experience. Occasionally a window shade would be pulled down, but otherwise there were only shadows behind glass windows. The narrow streets were deserted. At last I saw someone standing in a doorway—a woman with a scarf over her head—but she disappeared quietly.

*I don't think Liam had ever planned on meeting me,* I thought to myself. Then I remembered an interview in Dublin. I had talked to leaders of the Irish Republican Army. One looked over my identification papers carefully. "Sorry, but every time I meet an American, I think he's with the CIA," he laughed.

I had a terrifying thought. Maybe they lured me into this place for some other reason. I remembered the words of an Anglican priest. "I wouldn't put it past the IRA to kill an American just for the publicity."

There was no taxi, not even a telephone nearby. There was nothing I could do, so I decided I would go right into the tavern with all the bluff I could muster. The more I walked, the more confident I became.

*Don't be so paranoid,* I laughed to myself. *The Sinn Fein is paranoid, the cab driver is paranoid; you've got to keep your head.* I kept my eyes on the pavement as I walked.

*Actually, it is a good thing Liam didn't show up,* I thought. *By now, he would be rattling off quotes about job discrimination, British harassment, and lots of statistics. I can read the socialists' opinions in their own newspapers. If I want to see and hear what is really going on, I should go to the people themselves.*

Duggan's Tavern was just around the corner. There were about seven men at the bar. They were dressed in shabby clothes and some of them were unshaven. They were shouting, laughing, and drinking. Then I came in. My face appeared in a hundred bottles and mirrors. Silence fell like a guillotine. The men gave me a hostile glance that lasted only seconds, but it was effective. A skinny, middle-aged barmaid in a green sweater managed a weak, motherly smile.

I was not intimidated. I walked right to the bar. "Coca-Cola with ice." There was a roar of laughter. The bartender hesitated for a moment, looked me over, and disappeared into a back room. He returned with Coca-Cola, no ice, and I retreated to a bench against the wall. The talking and shouting resumed.

Everyone seemed indifferent to me. I reached for my notebook and started writing a description of the place. On the wall behind the barmaid was a picture of James Connally, an Irish nationalist executed by the British in 1916. Right next to it was a poster of Che Guevera. The walls were painted pink and red. There was an ugly linoleum on the floor. In the top corner of the room was a large new color television. They were watching a children's puppet show. Not exactly tavern entertainment, but there isn't much choice on Irish television.

At the bar, an old, gray-haired gentleman was the center of attraction. His bar stool was slightly superior to the others; it had a cushion.

The most ominous figures were two young men standing in the corner. They were in their late twenties. Unlike the others, they hadn't taken their eyes off me since I entered. Finally, they returned to their Guinness beer. They would glance up at the puppet show, take a sip of beer, and then glare back at me.

I got out my passport and press card. When I finished my Coke, I decided to go straight to them. One had long, greasy hair. He wore a blue suit, one size too small, and shiny from long wear. He wore black, pointed Italian shoes which looked like they'd been purchased in the 1960s and never polished since.

"I'm trying to get the story of what's going on here," I said, showing my identification. The bar was suddenly silent again. He looked at his friend and smiled. They were both a little surprised that I had approached them. His friend's name was Collins. Collins ran his fingers through his short, curly hair and said, "Ask him." He nodded to the old man down the bar, but the old man wouldn't talk.

That's when the barmaid came to the rescue. "Tell him 'bout the girl they shot last night."

"Oh, that happens all the time," a big fat man said.

"What happened?" I turned my tape recorder on.

The barmaid looked at it suspiciously for a moment and then went right ahead. "Well, a British soldier shot a young girl with a rubber bullet last night. It was at close range. She's a lovely girl, she is. Then he picked up the bullet so there would be no evidence. Happened right out here."

There were some groans of disappointment at that example. "That's nothing," someone said. Then the whole bar began to review some of the terror of the neighborhood.

"There was two murdered in this bar," the old man said, turning around on his stool. "I was sitting right back in that room."

Someone promised me a real live IRA leader who could "tell you plenty." He rushedout.

Then I met Sean. He was wearing a brown turtleneck sweater. His beard was trimmed handsomely and he was clean. He came over to talk.

"I can give you lots of stories. There was two young lads shot. One of them was shot dead."

My tape recorder was whirring. "Now these two boys that were shot—where was it?"

"Grosvenor Street."

"When did it happen?"

"Last, ah," there was a pause. "Sunday night," he said, as though he suddenly remembered, but several people in the bar corrected him. There was a big discussion trying to decide the exact time.

"I tell you what. You go down to his mother's, who lives on Merrion Street."

"Who do I ask for?"

"You will see Nugent."

"Yea, John Nugent," someone else chimed in.

"Is that the one who lost his son, or is that the one who lived?"

"No, that's the one who is critically ill," the old man interrupted, turning around on his barstool again.

Sean disappeared for a few minutes while I talked to the old man, but moments later our discussion was interrupted by a clatter of noise in a room behind the bar. Sean, the young man in the brown turtleneck sweater, signaled to me. "Here is a lady who will talk to you."

"She's coming in?"

"Yes. You see, I'll tell you what happened." Sean walked over to my table and leaned on it with both hands. "The British army started racking around here."

"By Duggan's Bar?"

"No, the whole district. The whole area. They racked up things pretty bad."

A short woman in her late fifties entered. They pulled up a chair for her, and she sat down opposite me.

"Something to drink," Sean called to the bartender.

"Oh, no, thank you," the woman interrupted in a high-pitched Irish voice.

"Do you know where the flats are up here?" Sean asked me.

"Yes."

"Her son was wandering through that place, so the British army asked him to halt, but he just walked on." There was a long pause. "So they opened fire on him."

The mother nodded her head. "He got away all right. He ran," she said excitedly.

"Did they shoot him with rubber bullets?"

"Oh, no! No!" Sean had a very serious look on his face.

Someone across the bar laughed loudly. "He's been reading the British press."

"They was real bullets, they were," the mother said meekly.

"Where did they hit him?"

"In the thigh."

When I asked how bad the wound was, she couldn't say.

"I haven't seen him for two days. My other son came rushing into the house. 'Oh, Mommy, they got him. They got him,' he said. 'Jimmy's shot dead.' "

"Did it scare you?"

"I thought he was dead." She started to cry.

For a few moments nobody said anything. I tried to think of something, but nothing would come.

"That same day the British army busted up her house," Sean said.

"Is that right?"

"They busted up my furniture. They pulled the lights out of the sockets."

"How much will it cost to fix it up?"

"It will never get fixed."

"Won't the British reimburse you?"

"No."

There was a long pause. The woman didn't seem bitter, just confused.

"My husband said, 'What about the furniture?' They told him to shut his mouth or they would take us all away."

"How old is your boy?'

"Twenty-five."

"It is hard to believe that the British army can do that."

"Oh, they do what they want," the barmaid said. "That happens all the time."

Sean squinted and looked out the window and across the street. "That's the same with internment. They put you in prison, but you are not charged with anything. They just say you are guilty."

"Happens here every night," the barmaid said again.

Sean suddenly had some inspiration. "You should come back here at night. Where are you staying?"

"The Europa Hotel."

"You ought to spend the night down here and see for yourself. You see, you just have our word. If you come back, you can see for yourself."

"Maybe Kitty O'Kane will take care of me."

"Oh, sure, someone would put you up."

I looked at my watch and then at my notes. "Well, how could I get down to John Nugent's house, the man whose son was just shot?"

"I'll take you."

I looked around to see Collins.

"Let's go," I said.

We got into an old blue van. Soon we were speeding through the narrow streets. When we turned the corner, something strange happened. Little children started screaming. Housewives and elderly women were running as fast as they could go. No one was looking back. It reminded me of my summer in East Africa: that magical moment when a lion enters the grasslands. In an instant, thousands of birds fill the sky, zebras are galloping away, the antelopes swish through the grass, and the monkeys chatter in the trees.

I turned around and looked down the street. It was a British lion. There was a patrol. An armored vehicle led the way, with soldiers on either side. Their faces looked hard; their jaws were firm. They carried machine guns. Their eyes darted from side to side. My driver hit the accelerator with a fury and made a screeching turn around the next corner, coming to a stop.

He was nervous, but he agreed to keep the motor running while I snapped some pictures. I looked around the corner. The patrol was moving up the street fast. They spotted me. Two of them pointed their guns at me. A gang of children came running down the street. Rocks and bottles flew through the air, but the patrol kept moving up the street. My driver couldn't delay any longer. He was off, leaving me surrounded by the British soldiers.

"What are you doing here?" one snapped curtly. "Give me some identification, quick."

"American press," I said.

He looked at my passport and ID. "You're crazy," he said. The patrol moved on by me.

I must have wandered through the neighborhood for five minutes before I found Collins surrounded by a group of soldiers. I turned the corner just in time to see him get slugged good in the mouth.

"Hey, that's my driver," I said, running toward the soldiers. I managed to talk them into confusion, which gave Collins time to pull out his identification papers. Perhaps they didn't want to look bad to a member of the American press; whatever the reason, they let us go.

"Why did they slug you?"

Collins was walking fast, but he didn't talk until we were at least a block away.

"Bastards! Now I've got to go back up there and get my truck. This could cost me my life."

I thought he was being a bit dramatic, but I didn't know. Who is Collins? Maybe the British know. Maybe they had some reason to rough him up. Maybe it was just because he was a Catholic.

"Wait right here," Collins commanded. I waited ten minutes. Just when I decided that I couldn't wait any longer, the blue van pulled up to the curb, and we raced off again. This time we drove without incident to Merrion Street. Collins stopped at Mr. John Nugent's house.

# 2

# Tonight They'll Kill a Catholic

No one leaves his home at night in the Falls Road area. But there are eleven children in the John Nugent family and they live in four rooms. So you can't blame a teen-ager for wanting to get out of the house.

Kierin, the fifteen-year-old, left the house at ten P.M. with his friend Barney McErilan. They were walking their dog to the corner. A car drove up. Two men fired machine guns. Barney fell to the sidewalk dead. Kierin was knocked ten feet. His body was slammed up against a stone wall. After taking eight bullets he collapsed to the pavement, too.

John Nugent welcomed me into his house immediately. "Sit here."

There was a ragged old couch with several children on it, but one section had a special cushion cover. It was the seat of honor. I sat down. A young woman sat to my left with children on her lap and on the arms of a big stuffed chair. To my right was more of the Nugent family. A fire burned brightly in a small fireplace. The room was half the size of my hotel room, with dirt on the floor. The children were wearing ragged clothes.

"Do you want some tea?" John Nugent offered.

"No, thank you. I want to talk to you about your son. They don't seem to write these stories in the American press."

John interrupted me. "I know. Yea, I know, but I'll tell you what it is, and I'll be truthful with you. The injustice of this place is this: I went through the last war, the whole of the last war. I collected nine medals. There they are up there." His thirteen-year-old son picked up a tin box from the mantle above the fireplace and opened the lid for me. John paused as I handled the medals. "I've never seen two lads shot up like them. They were riddled and ripped open with bullets."

"What did they shoot with?"

"They had a machine gun."

"A German what?" the woman asked. "A German Mauser?"

John was annoyed by the woman's interruption. "Aye, one of the German machine guns. The copper-topped ones."

"How old is your son?"

"He's fifteen. He's a schoolboy." John shouted it again, as if in disbelief that anyone would shoot him. "A schoolboy! A schoolboy!"

"He just stepped out of the house?" I asked.

"I was sitting right where you are watching TV there. He just put his head out and looked both ways. He and his chum were laughing at the robots."

"The robots?"

"On TV. You know—children's program. He said, 'Oh, dad, who would watch the robots?' Just kidding, you know, and the two of them walked the dog to the corner."

The little baby on the woman's lap started to cry.

"So they were at the corner of Merrion and Grosvenor Road?"

"Yea, and that is when the car drove up. They said, 'Come here, Nuge.' That means Nugent, you know."

"Were they British soldiers?"

"Oh, no, no. Wasn't. No, definitely not. They was two Orangies. Two bad . . . ."

I interrupted him. "Which group were they with, or do you know?"

"Uh, the U.V.F."

"The Ulster Vanguard Force?"

"Yea, that's them. That's who they were."

"But they knew his name, huh?"

"Oh, yea. They know all of us. They know me."

"What were they doing in this neighborhood?"

"They live in this neighborhood. They belong in this neighborhood."

"Were they arrested?" The question brought fire to John's eyes.

"There's a big fort over there, beside you there. Just across the road from where they got shot were two thousand soldiers, and they never got one of them. Only thing is, our Kierin lived to tell who done it to him. He says to me, 'Dad,' he says, 'I know who shot me,' and he says, 'you know him, too. Dad, I'm gonna tell you who shot me.' " John started talking very fast. "And he told the Special Branch, and he told the whole lot who shot him."

"You mean they didn't bring them into court?" I asked.

"Well, I think they've got them now."

The woman interrupted us. "They got them now," she said, "but they are not arrested."

Mr. Nugent's face had a helpless expression. "I haven't been notified officially that they got anybody for the shootin' of me son."

"Who was the boy that was with him?"

"His chum."

"What's his name?"

"Barney McErilan. They caught him. They cut poor Barney half in two."

"Did you hear the shots?"

One of the little Nugent boys began to simulate the sound of bullets. "Pop, pop, pop, pop, pop."

"Just like that," Mr. Nugent said. "They must have been about forty bullets fired. I jumped out right off."

"Where did they hit him?"

Nobody said anything. Mr. Nugent had tears in his eyes. Then the woman answered my question very slowly and very quietly. "Chest, arms, legs, back."

"Eight bullets taken out of him," John said. He walked over to the window and stared out. We were quiet. "Oh, they left him for dead."

"How many children do you have?'

"Eleven."

I turned to the thirteen-year-old boy who, throughout the interview, had displayed no emotion. "Where were you when your brother was shot?"

"I was upstairs. I ran down."

John walked back across the room. "He lifted Barney's head up, but poor Barney was dead straightaway. We was out on the street as soon as the first shots. I caught my son. They was still firing as they sped away."

"You were holding your son?"

"Yea. I carried him. Blood all over us. I don't know how I carried him. He's six-foot-three. He's a big, long fellow."

"What did you do with him?"

"I carried him back here, almost a block." Mr. Nugent started to cry. "I just held him in my arms. The blood was pumping out of his chest, out of his arms, out of his legs, all over. I laid him down right there, He says, 'Dad, I'm shot. I'm shot. Get me a priest.' "

"Sean got a man to drive him to the hospital," the woman said. "We were lucky that we were on time. He lost five pints of blood."

"How long was he in the hospital?"

"Oh, he's still in the hospital now," Mr. Nugent said. "Still going through an operation today. They have taken two bullets out of his back."

"When did it happen?"

"Tuesday, just a couple days ago."

"This happens often?"

"Oh," Mr. Nugent looked disgusted. "It's happening all the time."

"When will it end?"

"Well, uh," he smiled as though I was pretty naive.

The woman answered me. "I don't think it's ever going to end."

"It shouldn't have happened," John said, looking at one of his little boys.

"Why do you think they shot him? Why?"

"Well," John looked around the room as though he would catch the answer out of the air. "Just because he's Catholic," he said all of a sudden. "That's all."

"Don't you work? What about job discrimination?" I said, suddenly realizing that it was the middle of the afternoon. That question made him angry.

"Still the same. You can't get work." He was almost shouting at me. "I was a poor man anyway, but with a corporation, and I lost me job. They send you to work in the Protestant areas and you are pointed out just like that."

I looked around the room at the Nugent family and felt a little uncomfortable. I had just bought a new pair of shoes in Madrid. One of the little boys was looking at them. When I caught him, he smiled timidly.

But Mr. Nugent was worried about the children for another reason. He looked at his thirteen-year-old. The chubby, red-haired boy glared at the opposite wall. "I'll tell you what," John said. "They're driving people crazy here. The kids is hard and they're making you hard. You know what I mean like? There is stuff on both sides, I mean. Then you got a family who isn't bothering nobody and this happens."

"What happens here at night?" I said, wondering out loud.

"You can't even walk out that door." He was shouting again. "And when you pick up your bottle of milk in the morning, you're looking down that way and you're looking down this way."

Suddenly the door opened. Mrs. Nugent entered with her daughter. "This is Kierin's mother," John said. "This is a writer from America." She shot John a suspicious glance.

"Well, you'll get plenty to write about here," she said and disappeared into the kitchen.

John was nervous now. His wife probably didn't like the idea of her husband talking to a stranger. "The whole thing about it is this. There's nothing to hide. Everything's in order and above board. They come up to the two lads at the corner of the road, and it was cold-blooded murder. That's all it was. It was nothing but just dastardly, cold-blooded murder."

"But they have the two men?"

"Oh, we don't know. It's just a rumor, but you see, that's no good to me or me son. We already give them the names of the two that shot him."

"Will you ever know?"

John shrugged.

"If it was the other way around," the young woman said.

John interrupted her immediately. "Yea, if it was the other way around, you could throw a match on the street and be arrested and held under the Special Powers Act, yet two names was given to the security forces, as they call themselves here, that they shot me lad."

The woman seemed angry now. "And nobody has done anything about it," she paused, "but they had be better checking the men out."

John nodded vigorously. "You can say that again," he laughed, and his eyes got big. Then he excused himself and left the room.

He returned only moments later. He had a suit jacket on now with a hat in his hand. "I'm going to see Kierin now. I'll walk you to the corner."

I packed my tape recorder and headed for the door. "Thank you for the time," I called.

In spite of the strict orders that the mother gave from the kitchen, two of the little children followed along behind us.

Merrion Street is a lonely row of stone houses. It is much too narrow for parked cars. John and I walked the entire block. The sounds of children playing echoed from a nearby alley. On the other side of the street, a child stopped at a doorway. Right behind him was his mother. She wore a coat and had her purse in her hand, but when she saw me, she retreated back into her doorway immediately. Her child seemed delighted to see a new face. His eyes followed me with curiosity. I waved. The mother was not so pleased. I could hear her whispering frantically from the doorway. Finally, she grabbed his hand and jerked him back into the house.

At the corner of Merrion Street and Grosvenor Road, we stopped. Mr. Nugent showed me where the bullets had hit the wall. Some of the shots had ricocheted off the stone, leaving marks. Others had buried themselves. I stuck my little finger in a hole made by a bullet.

Grosvenor Road was busy compared to Merrion Street. Cars streamed by. Mr. Nugent had his hands in his pockets as he watched the traffic. He began to cry. Only Tuesday his boy lay in a pool of blood on this corner, but life went on here in Belfast.

"What would happen if the British left?" I asked.

"Oh, that would solve a lot of it. If they come around like they done the other night, there would be nothing left of them." He was suddenly excited again. "See, you can't even have a gun in your house with the British here. They are on top of you. I should have a gun in me house now, but if they come in, they tear up the whole house, and if they found a gun, they would take the whole lot away."

"Internment?"

"Yea."

"I thought they did away with internment."

"Well, it amounts to the same thing," John shrugged, somewhat distracted by my last statement. "If they'd get out, we could solve the things ourselves because the Irish should fight it among themselves anyway."

Mr. Nugent looked at his watch.

"Listen, you are going to be late," I said. "Thank you so much for the time."

"Oh, yea. That's all right."

"Here, I want you to have this." I gave him some money. I don't know why Americans think money is the solution to everything, but Mr. Nugent had taken certain risks in talking to me, and I was grateful.

"Thank you. Thank you." He was too proud to look me in the eye after that, but he took the money. "For the little ones, you know," he said looking down, and then he walked away.

I turned around and glanced back down Merrion Street. The mother and little son had been watching us, but she disappeared again when I looked her way.

There was another woman standing by her doorway this time. She was a heavyset, old woman, both hands on her hips, and she gave me a defiant glare. I decided to talk to her. She watched each step I took up the street. When I actually spoke to her, she became nervous.

"American press, huh?" She glanced at my identification suspiciously. Then she looked both ways down the street. After backing into her doorway, she agreed to talk.

"How do you feel about the situation here?" I asked.

"I feel rotten, that's how I feel. All the killing."

"Were you here when Kierin was shot?"

"Of course I was here. Everyone was here. It was ten o'clock at night. Everyone on the block looked out," she paused. "His daddy picked him up and carried him up the street. There was blood all over. The kids was screaming. Old Mr. Nugent was covered with blood, all over his suit and in his hair. The only place there wasn't blood was on his face where he was crying."

"Do you live by yourself?"

"Yes. I've lived on this block for forty years."

A priest walked by. The old woman didn't speak until she was sure he was gone. We watched him disappear up the street. When I turned around, I saw the Nugent boy again.

"This is Mary." He introduced me to a middle-aged woman holding a sack of groceries.

"You with American press?" she asked.

"Yes."

"You know, lots of what you read here isn't the truth." Her face flushed with anger as she spoke. "They had that in the paper that this street was all barricaded up. They said that no one could get in or out."

"Why would the paper print it if it wasn't true?"

"There wasn't a word of truth in it," she said painfully. "They don't write about the soldiers. They come up the streets and what they won't do."

But the old woman didn't think it was so bad. "They wrecking the doors is all I can see in this block."

"You've not had your house racked up yet," Mary said.

Not to be outdone, the old woman said, "I know what you're talkin 'bout. I had a friend that lived up on the other block." She leaned out of her doorway for the first time and pointed. "She was away on holiday. They broke into her place. Her watch was missing and everything."

"That's the army for you." Mary was angry. "Supposed to be protecting you. Did you hear about the big demonstration they had at City Hall? Them was Loyalists."

"I read about it in the paper."

"Do you think they would let us have a meeting? Oh, no. No."

"You should have been over here a long time ago writing your story," the old woman said. "What we're telling you is true."

Mary retreated as the Nugent boy whispered something in her ear. "I hope you is not with the Special Branch trying to get information out of us." Mary looked me in the eyes intently. "It takes us to watch what we are saying."

"He's got a tape recorder in there." The Nugent boy pointed to my coat.

There was an awkward moment of silence. My passport, press card, and any amount of reassurance did no good. The Nugent boy ran down the street. "I'll get help," he called back.

I started to walk the other way.

"And don't go around giving names to the enemy," Mary shouted, "because they'd catch you. You're never going to get back home again, you know."

"Okay." I acted calm, but my heart was beating fast.

"And watch your sayings down the road." She shouted more, but I didn't hear her.

*I stayed on the block too long,* I thought to myself. Where will I go now? I left Merrion Street and started down Grosvenor Road walking fast. A passing taxi reassured me. *I'll go back to Duggan's Bar and telephone for a driver.*

I was welcomed back to the tavern like a long-lost friend. There was a roar of approval when I told them that their side of the story would be told.

After making arrangements to get back to the Europa Hotel, the bartender signaled to me.

"Take over," he instructed another man. Then he disappeared into the back room with me close behind. We climbed the stairway. He fumbled with the key and finally opened the door to a long room. *Perhaps this is an inner sanctum of the IRA,* I thought.

There was a big table with chairs around it. There was an old carpet on the floor. The bartender walked over to the wall and glanced up at a painting.

"Well, what do you think of this?" It was a terrible oil portrait. The cheap frame didn't help much, but he was beaming proudly. "This is James Connally."

Connally was one of the revolutionaries who helped win freedom for the Irish Republic in the 1920s. Twenty-six counties were given independence in 1922. They formed the Irish Republic, but the six counties of Northern Ireland remained in the United Kingdom.

"Beautiful," I said.

The bartender wouldn't have cared if I was sincere or not. For a moment he seemed transfixed by the portrait. "Connally was born here in Belfast, you know."

He carefully locked the door when we left.

Downstairs, the crowd was quieter than usual. Tarzan was on television. I noticed Collins. His jaw was now swollen out of shape. I waited for the next commercial to say good-by.

Standing at the doorway with my cameras and tape recorder strapped over my shoulders, I wished them good luck. "A lot of people in America sympathize with your situation," I said to the whole bar. "We'll be praying for you."

Every head in the room turned to me in astonishment.

"We don't need prayers," Collins shouted back, with a wide grin on his face. "We need guns." Duggan's Tavern was filled with laughter.

# 3

# Tea at Margaret's

While I was working the Catholic side of the street, Roger Heuser, my research assistant, was spending the afternoon at the Ulster Defense Association headquarters. The UDA is the largest and most famous of the Protestant militant organizations. Its enemy is the IRA, and it has one all-important advantage: the UDA is legal, while the IRA is not.

The UDA vice-president, Tommy Herron, decided that Roger ought to visit a Protestant neighborhood. So he loaned him his brother-in-law as an escort and bodyguard. At first he didn't like the idea, but eventually he consented to help out.

They stopped in front of a long row of connected, quaint little homes about three blocks from a Catholic area. "You'll get a good interview here," Herron's bodyguard said.

He went to the door of a two-story house. No one was home. He looked around nervously before he returned to the car. "I have a price on my head, you know." Roger imagined that his escort was being dramatic, but he was wrong. A few weeks later the bodyguard was assassinated, and before the year ended Herron himself was brutally murdered.

Roger got out of the car. "Thanks. I think I'll look around the neighborhood by myself."

Rupert Stanley College was right across the street. It looked like any commuting college, mostly classrooms and little campus atmosphere. The students brushed by him in a hurry. The next class was about to begin.

One student stopped to talk. She remarked how she felt certain people get sadistic satisfaction out of reading violent news. She thought much of it was sensationalism.

However, the cleaning ladies in the college had different opinions. Within moments the halls were almost empty. Roger flashed his press card to the three with their buckets and mops, and turned on his tape recorder. They were flattered by his interest.

"Sure, we'll talk to you." They all laughed.

The first one started straightening her hair. She wanted to look her best for the tape recorder. "My husband worked on Grosvenor Road," she said. "When he came out through the gate, the Catholics met him and told him not to come back."

Another woman nodded sympathetically. "The Protestants' side isn't accurately being told." She leaned her mop against the wall. "If a Protestant gets shot, no one knows about it, no one hears the name. A Protestant could get shot in an alley and there wouldn't be a thing mentioned. The British army was brought in by only one segment of the population, and that was the Roman Catholics. Now they want them out. The problem wouldn't have been as bad if they had never been brought in. They've taken the British money, the Queen's money, and spendin' it."

The first woman had a simple explanation. "Devlin and Paisley started it all. There's no surrender. Her civil rights started the first spark. They're both equally as wrong. They're both to blame on both sides. It should get into a trial. Ireland was peaceful for fifty years. But then the Catholics started all this extremist stuff. They're scum."

"Not all of them are scum," the third lady said softly.

The first woman put her hands on her hips and looked Roger in the eye. "They're all scum!" she insisted.

Roger was feeling a little disappointed and frustrated at the Protestant image thus far. He left the college and walked hurriedly to a taxi station. The sun was disappearing, making the afternoon a little chilly. The echo of his steps added confusion to his cluttered head. Why all the apathy, hate, and indifference? The Catholic neighborhood was just ahead. He remembered the repeated warning of Tommy Herron's aide not to linger there. What would Catholics do if they found out that Roger was interviewing Protestants to get a good perspective of their feelings and hurt?

That's when he met Margaret. He almost knocked her over. She was scolding three young boys who were playing war in the debris of a bombed-out storefront.

Roger startled her when he accidentally bumped her armful of groceries. "Oh, I'm sorry! Excuse me."

When she heard his American accent, she lit up. "Oh, American press, I suppose! Well, come over to my flat for tea. I can tell you plenty."

It seemed strange that the old woman immediately trusted him. She walked off, confident that Roger had accepted her invitation. He smiled to himself and followed the old woman down the street.

As they walked together, Roger noticed one of her eyes was blind. She was short and heavyset, with graying hair. Her constant smile and witty humor was a welcome change.

They walked past a row of bricked windows and doors. Rolls of barbed wire prevented passage down the lane in back of the houses.

"Look up there," she pointed. "You'll see the houses, all burned and wrecked up. Them used to be Protestant homes." The old woman stopped and looked sadly down the block. "They never even had time to get their stuff out. They were all burned at one time!"

"When did this happen?"

"Last year it happened."

Roger took her groceries. "Let me help."

"Well, I could've carried me own things." She smiled shyly. But she kind of liked the idea.

The row of burned houses stretched four blocks long. They faced a school across the street. "The children have bomb scares every day of the week," she said excitedly. "Last week one of them went off! The children are frightened. The government pays ninety-five percent of the cost of private schools for Catholics. Still they want more from us. They build 'em big apartments and everything."

"Where are the families who once lived in these flats?" Roger asked, rotating his sack of groceries to the other arm.

"Some moved to another neighborhood, and some are on the run."

"Who bricked them up?"

"Oh, the British army," she said. "The IRA would get in. They like to shoot at people from the buildings and rooftops. Don't know if it does any good to brick'em up," she mumbled to herself. "A gunman was inside one just recently." There was fear in the lady's tired eyes. "You see what terror there is," she said.

They arrived at her small flat. There was a fireplace in the tiny living room. Margaret cleared the couch and Roger sat down. Then she disappeared into the kitchen.

Moments later the cheerful smell of hot tea and biscuits floated in. Roger looked at the old woman's coat which she had laid across a nearby chair. There was a pin on it.

"What's this pin on your coat?" he called to her. Then he read it carefully: BELFAST ORANGE WIDOWS OF NORTHERN IRELAND JUBILEE, 1921-1971.

Margaret appeared at the door of the kitchen. "Oh, that's my Orange Widows pin," she beamed proudly. "You're a Protestant, aren't ya?"

"Of course," Roger reassured her.

"Well, I knew ya was or ya wouldn't have taken my groceries and all."

"What does the pin mean?"

But the old woman didn't hear his question. She was staring off into space. Her thoughts were far away. "Northern Ireland's not the same as when I was young, when I was getting married. It's all changed. For years and years the Roman Catholics and Protestants mixed together. Nobody got hurt. They went here and there together, sat in bars together." The old woman sighed and returned to the kitchen.

"When did the trouble begin?" Roger called after her.

"1969," Margaret shouted back. "The IRA started shootin'. At night the young ones is out throwing bombs."

"In this neighborhood?" Roger asked.

"Yes," she shouted, and then she entered the living room with a tray. "There was a pub over here owned by a Protestant man. The pub was blown up and taken over by the Catholics. Now the Protestants can't go in there anymore." She sat down. "I remember when it was blown up. It knocked me out of me bed and onto the floor. How can I forget? It hurt me back, and I was bruised pretty badly."

"Do you have any close Catholic friends?"

"Before the trouble," she answered softly, "we were the best of friends. Now we'll pass each other by, and they'll not look or speak.

"Oh, it's bad," she said. "The IRA shoots at the Protestant boys coming home from church." Her hands were shaking badly as she poured his cup of tea.

"Here, I can do that," he said.

"It's awfully nerve-racking here." Margaret was embarrassed. "I tell you, our nerves are so bad that our very hands an' everything shake. But we're staying here."

Margaret has a daughter in Canada who wants her to move there, but she refuses to leave. "There's only a few of us left." She shook her finger in Roger's face. "I don't care if they blow my house up in the air. I'll go up along with it before I leave."

Margaret showed Roger the kitchen where she sat in fear and bewilderment while they broke the front windows of her house. They had been broken four times by rocks, bottles, and gunfire.

"The kitchen is the safest place," she spoke in a whisper as though someone might overhear her. They sat down and Roger listened with amusement as she explained her theory. The old woman had paced through her entire flat before arriving at her conclusion. Now she retreated to the kitchen in times of trouble.

"Don't get it in your head that we're afraid of these Catholics, 'cause we're not!" she shouted. "We're going to stay until we go up in the air! Keep your head up. We're still here! Ulster will be Ulster while we're able to hold it. We'll never give it up!" She clenched her fist.

Roger glanced out the window and realized that it was getting late. The sun was setting fast now. The time had gone by quickly. As he got up to leave, Margaret's enthusiasm faded. She sat quietly, but he could feel her disappointment.

"It's not easy to live alone at nights in this neighborhood," she said bravely.

Her new friend had to leave. Margaret got up and walked into the living room. She took the pin off her coat and handed it to Roger. He hesitated, but she insisted.

"Cover it up. Don't let anyone see it," she warned. "You're not even allowed to wear your own colors anymore. Get back if you can, but I might never see you again. For God's sake, tell them not to blame it on us. We get blamed on everything. Nothin' gets told. There was an explosion last night that was never published."

Roger looked at the serious expression on her face and smiled. He thought of his own mother and put his arms around the old woman to hug her tightly.

She just stood there for a moment. Roger opened the door.

"And don't believe what you sees on the telly," she said, following him out into the night. "The BBC and the Ulster TV are rotten to the core. I wouldn't speak three words to them. They're nothing but propaganda for the IRA."

She grabbed his arm. "The sooner you get out of this country the better. And maybe when everything is settled you can come back again. And if this street's still here, you can visit me. There's not a night of sleep that you don't hear shootin' from that end." She pointed down the street toward the Catholic neighborhood.

Roger started to leave her again, but she gripped him tighter. "Be careful now where you're goin' and what you say. And when the war is over and you come back, we'll give you a party."

# 4

# Ian Paisley Doesn't Believe It

I met the Reverend Ian Paisley in the coffee shop of the Europa Hotel. He is a big man with a soft voice. Not only does he pastor a local Free Presbyterian church, but he also serves as a member of British Parliament. He is probably the most famous anti-Catholic in the world.

I wasn't sure how to approach him. Another of my assistants, David Womersley, had suggested we talk religion with Paisley. I was writing an article for *Christian Life* magazine that week, so I decided to try.

"I'm from *Christian Life*—." He didn't wait for me to finish.

"Oh, that's Billy Graham's magazine," he said with disgust.

"No," I corrected him. "But occasionally it does a story about him."

"Are you an evangelical or a fundamentalist?" He looked at me suspiciously.

I was a bit surprised at how easily he divided Protestant Christianity into two camps. It is not good enough to be a Protestant. You have to be a fundamentalist.

I knew what the right answer was. "I'm a fundamentalist," I said. Then he seemed to open up.

"You should've been in my church Sunday night."

"I heard about it," I answered. A reporter from the *Baltimore Sun* had been there. Paisley had preached against "idolatry in the Catholic church."

Our conversation was interrupted. Roger Heuser came rushing into the coffee shop with a tape recorder. His long hair gave the Reverend a start.

"He's not a fundamentalist, is he?" He turned to Roger, who had just sat down. "You wouldn't say you're a fundamentalist, would ya?"

Roger looked at me in bewilderment.

"He's an evangelical," I said with a mischievous smile.

Paisley was relieved. A long-haired fundamentalist might be difficult to reconcile. "Evangelical," he said. "Emphasis is on the *geli*." He started preaching to Roger, who turned to me with a what-have-I-done-now look on his face.

"Even Bishop Robinson calls himself an evangelical," Paisley stormed. "Honest to God. The pope claims he's an evangelical. I find that the term *evangelical* covers a multitude of sins. When I say I'm a fundamentalist, people know that I believe in the virgin birth and in the inspiration of Scriptures."

Paisley's obsessive anti-Catholicism began to receive international attention during the late 1960s. When Northern Ireland's former prime minister, Captain Terence O'Neill, attempted to achieve reconciliation between the two sections, Paisley opposed him. He preached against him in his pulpit. He led angry mobs in the chant, "O'Neill must go!"

When Anglican Archbishop Ramsey received an invitation to visit the pope, an airlift was organized to Rome to demonstrate and pass out anti-Catholic literature. When Dr. Moorman, the bishop of Ripon and an Anglican observer to Vatican II, was invited to speak in Belfast, it had to be canceled. It was said that Paisley threatened to send his people into the streets to picket.

More recently, people have noticed a "new Paisley." "He appears to have changed since he has been elected to British Parliament," says an Anglican priest. "In his TV appearances he seems to be a highly responsible person. In many cases, he does talk an awful lot of sense. But I think people ought to remember the sort of person he used to be."

"He's the bravest man in Northern Ireland," says a Belfast taxi driver. "I'll bet he's the number one target for assassination in Ulster. But he don't scare easy. No bodyguards like the others. Nothin'."

Now I sat across from the man myself. "We've been down on the Falls Road," I said. "And I have heard some terrible stories. The internment policy . . . ." I was interrupted.

"Well, I was opposed to internment."

Roger sat up. "You were?"

"Oh, yes. Because internment was a sad thing. The government didn't use the due process of the law and then suddenly said, 'We're going to intern ya.' Well, naturally the majority of the people interned were going to be Roman Catholics."

This was the new Paisley talking. He had taken certain risks in opposing internment, which was very popular with most Protestants.

"The Catholics say that the detention-without-trial policy is really the same thing," I said.

"Oh, no. They can have a lawyer. They are allowed to show evidence."

My afternoon with John Nugent was still fresh in my mind. "I met a man whose son was shot a few days ago," I said. "They claim they know who did the shooting."

Paisley immediately closed his eyes tightly and started shaking his head. It looked as though he didn't want to hear what I was saying. "I don't believe it," he kept mumbling under his breath.

Was he disputing my facts? I continued, "The assassins are members of some Protestant militant group, but nothing has been . . . ." Once again I was interrupted.

"I don't believe it." He shook his head again. It was as if he'd heard it all before, and he already knew that the story I was starting to tell was untrue. "I mean, the Whitelaw administration has been very hard on Protestants. Sometimes evidence against Protestants has been falsified. Protestants have even been harassed to try and show that we're British. We're sympathetic to both sides.' "

We both looked at him and said nothing.

"I mean, you can't run a country in a state of turmoil like this," he continued. "You can't say we've harassed one Roman

Catholic and now we must find a Protestant. It's not right."

Suddenly he was up. "It's time for my appointment upstairs," he explained. "Would you like to walk along with me?" We followed to the elevator and down the tenth-floor corridor, talking all the way. And then he was gone, leaving us with dozens of questions yet to explore.

Roger left for an appointment in East Belfast with Mr. McCreedy, head of the Loyalist Association of Workers.

McCreedy was eager to talk. "We work with the political parties who are upholding the Constitution of Northern Ireland."

"And why do you feel this has to be?" Roger asked. "Isn't there equality between the two segments?"

"Of course, there's equality amongst the two sections. There's no doubt about that. You know," Mr. McCreedy began, "I haven't found any Roman Catholic yet who can tell me how they've been discriminated against. I mean they've had the same opportunities as what the working-class Protestant people have had. To my mind, there's no discrimination whatsoever against 'em. They've been given new homes over the past lot of years, just the same way as Protestant families have been getting new homes." He leaned back in his chair and looked out the window. "You take the Ballymurphy Estate, for example. Before one Roman Catholic family moved in there, it was a picturesque estate, brand new houses, fresh paint on the doors. Have a look at it now."

"What's it like now?" Roger asked.

"Well, they've used their front doors to burn in their fires. The place is like a pigsty," McCreedy said bitterly. "It's like a mire."

"Was it really nice?"

"When it was first built, which was about ten years ago. Now it's a slum . . . an IRA stronghold. There's only two out of ten working. All the rest are on Social Security benefits."

"Why?"

"They're too lazy to work," McCreedy answered, as though

it should be obvious. "They don't want to work. But they scream 'Discrimination!' "

"Have any of the Protestant workers you represent been discriminated against or harassed by the Catholics at all?"

"Of course they have!" His eyes widened. "They have been forced out of their homes! They have been burned out of their homes! They've been discriminated against in their places of work!"

"How have they been discriminated against in their places of work?" Roger asked.

Mr. McCreedy bit his lower lip. "Well, they've been told to get out or they'll be shot."

"Who is the majority and who is the minority in places like that?"

"Well, you see, you take any company or business in the town over this past number of years. It has become so that either Protestants or Catholics have dominated every factory and every company throughout Northern Ireland. It used to be at one time that there was Catholic and Protestant workers within every factory. Then slowly pressures were put on from either side, whereby it became predominantly Protestant or Catholic. This is the situation we have now."

"You said that before they used to be equal?"

"Oh, yeah. Catholics have never been discriminated against in this country as far as work is concerned, or homes have been concerned, or Social Security benefits have been concerned."

"But the Catholics do discriminate against the Protestants?"

"Not only now." McCreedy lowered his voice. "This has started ever since the troubles began. We're not saying that it doesn't happen on both sides. We like to be honest and fair. But you've got to look at the situation overall to find that there are many innocent Protestants who have been involved in this conflict. Many innocent Protestants have been shot down from IRA gunmen walking along the street. There are many families who feel bitter because they've had sons and daughters murdered by IRA terrorists."

"Do you see a compromise between the two ever?"

"No, we'll never have that. Because for one reason—their

two policies don't come anywhere near each other. The UDA are dedicated to defeat the IRA," McCreedy said. "The IRA are dedicated to defeat the Constitution."

"And who do you think will win?"

Mr. McCreedy looked Roger in the eye. "The UDA. If it comes to a crunch between the Protestant UDA and the Catholic IRA, the UDA will win, because the IRA are animals and the UDA are not."

McCreedy waited for Roger to say something, but he didn't. So McCreedy continued, "There's only one thing you do with an animal when it turns nasty. You put it down."

"When will this happen?"

"Well, this is something that we have maintained all along. This isn't something that will happen overnight. The IRA have been using guerrilla warfare tactics for some time now, and they will probably continue doing that. But between the security forces on the ground and the UDA in the background they will eventually be defeated. Not that I can speak for the UDA. I am speaking mainly from the LAW point of view. But, as I say, the UDA and the LAW are very closely linked."

Perhaps the most fascinating interview of the day came moments later at UDA headquarters. We met with Tommy Herron again. Herron was a favorite of foreign journalists, who felt that he could easily be provoked into fiery statements. Ironically, by Irish standards he was considered a moderate. When his dead body was found in a ditch near Lisburn later in 1973, the murder was blamed on a rival Protestant group who thought Herron was "soft on Catholics."

"Mr. Herron, you have been quoted as suggesting that the British have been harassing your organization."

He took a long drag on his cigarette and turned to an assistant nearby. "Well, there's a glaring example there. When's the last time you stopped in your own house?"

"Oh, about three months ago, approximately," the man replied nervously.

"Tell him why," Herron's face flushed with anger.

"The army, the security forces is after me. There's no way I'm safe."

Herron turned to us. "I met a corporal in the 35th Engineer Regiment who said that he would personally make mincemeat out of him when he gets his hands on him."

"Why?" we asked.

Herron threw his hands up in the air. "I don't know. Just because he's with the UDA."

He took another long drag on his cigarette before he squashed it in the ashtray on his desk. "This is part of the reason we say it's harassment," he continued. "I personally went to both police stations and spoke to both chiefs of police. They said they didn't want Mr. Treety in connection with any criminal activity whatsoever. However, they said they couldn't speak for the army, but they would try to find out. So they called back and forth and found nothing out about Mr. Treety because he hasn't violated any laws."

"He still cannot come back to his own house?"

"That's correct. I brought the case personally to Mr. Whitelaw," (secretary of state for Northern Ireland) "but we haven't got any word back. This was about a week ago." Herron started nervously tapping his desk with his pencil. "He's got four children."

Roger turned to the tall man standing against the wall. "What about your family, Mr. Treety?"

"They're kicked out of bed at four o'clock in the morning to find out where their dad is."

"This happens every morning?"

"Yes, sir. For seven days a week they got them out of bed at all different hours. They get them up and then ask them questions about their daddy." Mr. Treety sat down and lit up a cigarette.

"Is this a Protestant neighborhood?"

"Yes," he answered meekly. "And I also have a son who's been in the hospital for a month and I've never been able to see him."

"Why?"

"The security forces never let me."

Tommy Herron shifted uncomfortably at his desk. He glared at Mr. Treety for a moment and then nervously took another cigarette himself.

"Are they after you for something?"

Herron answered for him. "We tried to clear this up when we asked the local police if they wanted him. They said categorically, 'No, we don't want him. He's done nothing as far as we're concerned.' "

"Mr. Herron, what is the UDA all about?"

"The purpose of the UDA is as its name states, Ulster Defense Association." There was a long pause. "However, sometimes we have to take the offense."

"When would you consider taking the offense?"

"Well, when we locate known terrorists or their hideouts, or when we find strategic targets across the border."

"Are there any outside forces here?"

"Yes. There are bounty hunters who get £500-1,000 for the soldiers they kill. They are imported by the IRA. Some are from Belgium; some are from France." Herron smiled as he saw the look of surprise on Roger's face. "You see, the IRA are not for the Catholic people. They oppress the Catholics. There was an explosion planned by the IRA in which seven Catholics were killed at a customs post in Derry. They had no qualms at all and claimed it was their work. And this is freedom for the Catholic people?" His smile widened. "If they are their friends, God help their enemies."

"Is there any way in which this story of Northern Ireland is misrepresented by the press?"

Herron didn't wait for Roger to finish. "I think the conflict is not as sectarian as it appears," he answered eagerly. He glanced at Mr. Treety and then coughed in his own cigarette smoke. "I don't think anyone has anything against Catholics or Protestants. On either side I think it's anarchy."

A few days later the newspapers reported a power struggle within the UDA. Tommy Herron's brother-in-law was brutally murdered and Herron himself thrown out of power.

Months later, on September 14, 1973, Herron disappeared after attending a meeting at UDA headquarters in East Belfast. His body was found in a ditch the following Sunday. He had been shot in the head.

UDA sources suggested that he had been murdered by a

splinter group of the extremist Ulster Volunteer Force (UVF), whose members were angry over Herron's moderate ideas.

After spending several days interviewing various Protestant leaders, Roger, David, and the others on the research team met in my hotel room. We listened to hours of our tape cassettes.

"Did he say 'animals'?" I asked when the McCreedy tape was played.

"Yes—and he's not the only one who called the Catholics 'animals,' " someone answered. We played back a conversation he had recorded. It was an interview with the doorman of the YMCA.

"The trouble is communism. There's no doubt about it," the doorman had said. "The Catholics don't want peace in this country, so where's the answer? The Catholics are animals."

We sat for a moment without a word. He rewound the tape.

*So where's the answer? The Catholics are animals.*

We were silent. I think at that moment we were beginning to understand the degree of hatred in Northern Ireland. Once more he played the tape.

*So where's the answer? The Catholics are animals.*

# 5

# Colonel Sillitoe

Roger and I were having supper with Chris Little, a photographer on assignment for *Time* magazine. Roger was busy telling about the terrified Protestants he had been interviewing. I was convinced that any injustice in Northern Ireland was at the expense of the Catholics. Chris Little was unimpressed with both of our arguments.

"What about the British soldiers?" he asked. "They're the ones getting shot. They're in the middle."

Chris told us about a day he had spent with the army. He had worn a British uniform and followed a foot patrol into the Ardoyne.

"Thev have a good intelligence network here," he said softly, leaning into the table.

"Who?"

"The IRA," he answered. "When I was with the British army in the Ardoyne, a group of little kids came around the corner. I had never seen them before. One of them shouted 'Chris Little, we're going to get you!' "

Roger sat up. "How did they know your name?"

Chris shrugged and looked around the elegant hotel dining room. "They know everything that goes on here. They may have agents planted in this hotel. They know everyone who comes and goes."

"I'd like to talk to some army brass," I said.

"Well, don't ask to go on a patrol. It's dangerous," Chris warned.

The next day I was in touch with the British army headquarters in Lisburn. I told them I wanted an interview. They arranged for me to meet Lt. Col. Warren Sillitoe, the senior press officer, at two-thirty.

I arrived three hours early. I thought they might give me someone to interview.

The guard at the gate didn't ask for any identification. He didn't even search my Air New Zealand flight bag, which was strange. Getting into my own hotel was much more of an ordeal—you were herded into a little shed twenty yards from the entrance, frisked, and had your bags searched. Not at army headquarters. If they had looked in the bag, they would have found a camera, a notebook, and a tape recorder. But I could have as easily been carrying a bomb.

I walked fifteen yards to the main building of the army headquarters complex. Once again, I reached a checkpoint. This time I was stopped, my identification was carefully scrutinized, but again, no one checked my bag.

A tall guard walked me down a long corridor to the press room.

The walls were covered with maps. A large map of Belfast caught my attention. The Catholic and Protestant areas were blocked out with special colors. I glanced at Antrim Road, where only a few days ago four British soldiers had been lured into an apartment and had been machine-gunned by the IRA.

I pulled out my camera and started taking pictures of the room. The press officers were congenial and relaxed.

"Where's the colonel?" I asked.

A soldier looked at his watch and then the clock on the wall. "He's attending the special memorial services for the soldiers who were shot on Antrim Road. Should be back." As he spoke, Lieutenant Colonel Sillitoe walked in.

"What's he doing here?" the colonel motioned to me.

Before the soldier could answer, I tried to explain. "I had an appointment with you at two-thirty," I told the colonel. "But I thought . . . ."

He interrupted me, "And what are you doing here now?" He scowled at the other officers. "I'm going to listen to the news and I want it quiet!" He turned to me. "Then I'm going to eat lunch, do some paperwork, and I will not be able to see you until two-thirty as arranged."

Another soldier gave me a sympathetic look as he poured a cup of coffee. "Want something to drink?"

Lieutenant Colonel Sillitoe turned the dial on the tiny portable radio.

When the news came on, we listened to an announcer recount the details of the murdered soldiers. Sillitoe stared out the window as he listened. Then we heard a description of the memorial services. He turned off the radio.

"The French television people are here," someone said. "They want to know if they can set up their cameras in the other room."

"What's wrong with this room?" the colonel answered quietly.

"They felt it would be easier."

"Better lighting," someone else added.

The colonel nodded permission. He seemed annoyed by my presence.

"You can join me for lunch," he said quickly, and then started out the door. At first I wasn't sure that he was even talking to me, but I grabbed my flight bag and raced out the door after him.

We marched quickly down the corridor. Sillitoe was older, but I had to do an occasional double step to keep pace with him.

"This is my third trip to Northern Ireland this year," I said eagerly. "So far, most of the material I've gathered has been from a Catholic or Protestant viewpoint." I paused, but the colonel didn't say anything. "That hasn't been intentional," I continued. "I tried to contact Major Rovjent on a previous trip."

A passing officer saluted. We walked through the main doors of the headquarters building and out into the sunshine.

"Go on," the colonel said.

"Well, I'm leaving for Dublin in a few days. Then back to the

United States. I want to get the British side of the story. Frankly, I haven't been able to get any help from the army."

Then Colonel Sillitoe started talking. It was amazing. I guess he gets asked the same questions all the time because he proceeded to answer all the questions I had in mind. He was probably the most articulate man I interviewed in Northern Ireland. Unfortunately, he wouldn't let me record our conversation.

"You've heard that we harass Catholics. Well, I'll tell you what must be considered is the fact that 199 soldiers we know were killed by Catholic gunmen. Only two by Protestants. Yes, we will search the Catholic areas for guns as long as they're the ones doing the killing."

I told him about John Nugent's boy.

"If they want the soldiers to leave, there is a simple solution," he countered. "If they will put down their guns and live in peace with each other, we will go home."

We entered the officers' bar. It was crowded with newsmen and soldiers. We picked up a plate lunch and moved over to a couch.

The colonel was a perfect specimen of the proud, professional soldier. He was forty-three years old, but he stood tall and his face was handsome.

"Explain something to me," I said. "The soldiers I have interviewed downtown seem timid and shy. Some of them seem like frightened little boys. But the soldiers I saw in the Falls Road area were alert and brave. They were in great danger, yet they seemed to have more confidence than the men in the safe area."

The colonel had just taken a big bite of his sandwich, so I had to wait until he awkwardly chewed enough of it to talk again.

"They're fulfilled," he said with his mouth still full. I guess he wanted to give me a preview of what his answer would be. He took a big gulp of beer. "They're fulfilled as soldiers. This is what they were trained for. I would go crazy working with boys back in England. I am a soldier," he said proudly. "This is what I was trained for."

I told him about Chris Little, the man from *Time*. He was angry about the idea of putting a civilian in a British uniform.

"If that's true, it won't happen again!" he said.

I noticed a curious delight when I told him about the children in the Ardoyne.

"Oh yes, they've got quite an intelligence network," he said with a chuckle. I got the impression that as a military man he was proud of professionalism, even the enemy's. Sillitoe later insisted that this impression was wrong.

"Ian Paisley told me that the army has been prejudiced against the Protestants," I said, "just to prove that they aren't biased against Catholics."

Sillitoe straightened up. "We are fearless of criticism from either side."

"Can I quote you?" I got out my note pad.

He took another drink of beer. "We are fearless of criticism from either side," he repeated very seriously.

"Why would a British soldier have slugged my driver in the Falls Road area?"

The colonel's eyes widened. I told him about the incident with Collins. He gave me a very good explanation, but I was still troubled by some of the stories I had been told by Catholics the day before. The more questions I asked, the more tense the atmosphere became.

"I tell you what I'm going to do, Mr. Wead. I'm going to send you on a patrol and let you feel what it's like to be a soldier for a day. Maybe that will answer a lot of your questions."

It took approximately fifteen minutes to arrange things. Sillitoe gave some orders to a nearby officer and then made a phone call to Lt. Peter Ward. I could hear only portions of the conversation. . ."do this as a favor to me. . .he hasn't seen the British . . . ."

Moments later I was in a taxi riding back into Belfast. *That's strange,* I thought to myself. Lieutenant Colonel Sillitoe had said it would take me fifteen minutes to get a taxi. This man was waiting for me at the army headquarters entrance.

Then I realized. I was not in a taxi at all. There was no meter. It was just a plain car. *Maybe he wants money,* I thought.

"How much will this cost?" I asked out loud.

The driver looked at me in the rear view mirror. "Fifty pence."

That puzzled me. My ride out from Belfast was more expensive. "Are you sure you know where the Glen Ravel Street RUC station is?" I asked. (RUC stands for Royal Ulster Constabulary.)

"I know where it is."

Then I knew what had happened. The IRA had picked me up. They monitor all taxi calls. Sometimes they send their own cars.

My driver circled Belfast for two hours and then dropped me off miles from Glen Ravel Street Station. "It's just around the corner up there," he said, pointing to an old apartment building. Then he sped away.

I don't know what would have happened if I had walked to that corner. Instead, I spotted a passing army patrol and flagged them down. "No, there's not an RUC station near here," a corporal told me. "You're miles from the Glen Ravel Street."

"I had an appointment with Lt. Peter Ward thirty minutes ago," I explained.

They radioed in to headquarters to check out my story. Within minutes I was hustled across town in a military police car.

Lieutenant Ward met me at the Glen Ravel Street RUC station.

"Mr. Wead?"

"Yes."

"Let's go, I'll take you to your patrol."

I jumped into the front seat of his car and we were off.

"Sorry for the trouble," he said.

"I'm getting used to trouble," I mumbled.

"Yes. Well, let me give you a little briefing. You're going to be on a foot patrol in the New Lodge Road area," the lieutenant explained. "It is a Catholic area, and it will be dangerous. Your patrol is with the 42nd Commando Royal Marines. They arrived here February 14, 1973, from Plymouth."

We were interrupted by a radio call. While the lieutenant talked, I reloaded my tape recorder and camera.

It took us ten minutes to rendezvous with the patrol. We

were on a back road when we found them. There were four soldiers. Behind them was a school playground.

"This is an American writer," Lieutenant Ward explained. "He is going to go on patrol with you. He will ask you some questions about what you are doing."

"We just come from the Unity flats," Corporal Timms answered.

"Well, go through them again," the lieutenant commanded. "The colonel wants him to get the feel of the British foot patrol."

Then he sped away.

# 6 On Patrol with the British Army

Most of the soldiers who die in Northern Ireland are ambushed while on foot patrol. The very object of the foot patrol is draw fire—to be a walking target in an IRA stronghold.

The soldiers crouched against the playground fence. Their eyes darted from rooftop to rooftop. Corporal Timms had not looked Lieutenant Ward in the eye once during their short conversation. Instead, he was looking up and down the street.

All I could see was a deserted street and, behind us, a playground of little children.

"Let's go," the corporal said, and we trotted down the street toward some apartments.

"Where are we going?" I asked.

"Unity flats," someone answered.

It looked like a complicated military ballet as they moved through the maze of apartments. The soldiers would stand, then crouch, sometimes run. They had an amazing rhythm. When they could, they would stay close to the walls. When we reached a corner, their muscles tensed.

I felt awkward walking along beside them taking pictures. Once a little boy came racing around a corner on his tricycle and almost knocked me over. He was followed by a cluster of girls and boys. They stopped when they saw me.

"Hey, take my picture, mister."

I did. That was a mistake. We were followed by dozens of little children for ten minutes. "Take my picture, too, mister."

Corporal Timms spotted a woman with a basket under her arm. He muttered something softly, and she came over to him. He was very polite, but he wanted to search her.

The other soldiers went into action immediately. One raced down to the corner to give coverage while he searched the woman.

"They use women as their gunrunners," one of the soldiers explained. "They caught a woman over here the other day, didn't they, John?" he looked over to his companion.

"There was three thousand rounds and a couple revolvers," John answered.

"Where was this?" I asked in amazement.

"In her house, Stratheden Street, not far from here."

"What's the most dangerous part of your patrol?"

"This right here, Unity flats. Yesterday they found seven rifles and a couple of shotguns in these flats."

"Have you ever seen anyone shot?"

"Couple days ago."

"What happened?"

But there wasn't time for me to find out. Corporal Timms signaled and we were off again.

Sometimes I walked with the leader. He has the permanent job of scouting ahead of the other three. Sometimes I dropped back to Steve, the last soldier. He reminded me a lot of a cousin of mine with the same name. He was handsome in his uniform. Sometimes I got the impression he was purposely posing for some of my photographs.

"What is the purpose of the foot patrol?"

"To get shot at," he answered.

I didn't say anything.

"No, I'm serious," Steve said. "We draw fire. That's why they send us out—to get shot at. Then the corporal calls in for help from the mobile units. It's the only way we can draw them into a fight."

"Look out!" the corporal yelled.

We were walking down an alleyway with walls on either side.

A barrage of rocks and bottles came raining down on top of us. A milk bottle smashed to the brick street right next to me and sent glass flying across the road. We stopped and leaned against the walls. My heart was pounding fast.

"Where's it coming from?" Steve asked. No one answered him. The corporal was busy talking on his radio.

"Have you ever been shot at?" I asked Steve.

"No, I just got here." I noticed perspiration on his neck, even though it was a cold March afternoon. "Ask him," he nodded toward John.

I pulled out my tape recorder and turned to John. "Someone was shot the other day, you were telling me."

"On Lepper Street, just over here," he answered.

"What happened?"

"Young soldier was shot in the stomach. I didn't see it happen. I heard about it. There was this Catholic girl, about thirteen. She was laughing and dancing around. 'They got him,' she said over and over. 'They got 'im! They got 'im!' And there was these two blokes standin' there smilin', lookin' down."

Once more John's story was interrupted. The corporal gave the call, and we were off. I looked around the corner where the rocks and bottles had come from. No one was in sight except one old man. He was standing out in the street, hunched over with his hands in his pockets. I'll never forget the look on his face. I have never seen a face communicate that much hatred. Yet in a way it intrigued me. I let the soldiers walk on ahead and I lingered to see if he was actually giving me that look. He was. He glared at me, and I knew he hated me. Why? Because I was walking with the British soldiers?

After circling through the Unity flats, we returned to the schoolyard where I had joined the patrol. The children were having afternoon recess. A lively game of soccer was going on one end of the field.

We wound our way up a narrow street toward Antrim Road. A baby sat in a carriage in front of a doorway. I had a good idea for a picture, so I raced ahead with my camera. I planted myself across the street from the patrol. One by one the soldiers with their heavy, bulletproof vests and rifles moved past the little baby. I snapped a dozen pictures.

When we reached Antrim Road, the sounds of the school playground were overtaken by the trucks and buses that roared by. It felt good to see a lot of faces on the street. *That was quite an experience,* I thought to myself. I had the eerie feeling that we had been watched throughout our tour of the Unity flats. Now I felt safer.

"On the roof!" Corporal Timms shouted in an almost hysterical voice. He pointed to the house across the street. The soldiers disappeared around a corner.

I froze. My pulse was beating like a drum in my head. I thought of a lot of things in those few seconds. I saw Corporal Timms aim his rifle. *I can't follow them around the corner or I might get hit in crossfire. . .I shouldn't run back to the other corner—it's too far . . . the gunman may shoot at me on impulse . . . maybe he'll think I'm an Army photographer.* A big, red double-decker bus rolled by. A man inside was reading a newspaper, unaware of the tension he was riding through. Mostly, I remember the sidewalk. I could describe that sidewalk in great detail. I wondered if it would be the last sight I would ever see.

In the background I could faintly hear Corporal Timms calling to me. It had all happened in a few seconds. Finally I decided to make a run for it. My camera and tape recorder were dangling from my shoulder and some of my notes fell to the ground. But I ran.

"Hold your fire, men!" the corporal shouted.

I raced around the corner and leaned in as close to the wall as I could. Steve was clutching his rifle. He was gasping for breath, too.

"Did you see him?" he asked.

"Listen up, men!" the corporal shouted. I stuffed my notes and camera back into my Air New Zealand flight bag. "We're gonna' move straight across the road. Straight to Thorndale. The alley. All right? Stand by!"

They ran across the street toward the house. This time I didn't want to get stranded by myself. I raced after them. There was a loud crack from a rifle. I saw them disappear around the corner of the house. Charging down the sidewalk, I almost ran into a young woman with her baby.

I found them in a narrow alley behind the house. "Did you see him?" I asked Corporal Timms.

"Yeah."

"Was that a shot I heard?"

"Don't know. You can never be too careful."

I felt good at the prospect that there may not have been a shot at all. Maybe a car backfired.

The other three soldiers were leaning aginst a damp wall with their guns poised. Steve was still panting. "It was a shot, all right," someone whispered.

The alley was very narrow and dark. We were between two brick walls with cut glass and barbed wire on top of them. It was getting colder. The afternoon sun was shielded by the tall, stone houses that fronted Antrim Road. Corporal Timms was standing beside a wooden plank that was laid like a bridge from the wall to a second-story window of a house.

"He's in there. You can see where he's gone in. There onto the plank and into the house. Then out through the roof. The roof is smashed anyway."

Some children ran by us down the alley. A little boy stayed behind. Finally he crouched down between John and Steve.

"Timms!" John called.

"Yeah?"

"He's been there all week, according to this kiddie."

"Yeah. There's someone in there."

"What will you do now?" I asked.

"We haven't enough men to go in," Corporal Timms answered, "so I radioed to a mobile unit."

"Could he get away on the other side?"

"No. It's boarded up in the front. He will have to come back across this plank. An' we're waitin' for 'im. Only thing," the corporal looked at the roof, "he could've jumped over to the next house." Then he turned to the others, "I'm goin' to scout a bit up the alley."

"Okay," John answered. The corporal jogged away.

We sat quietly for five minutes. The soldiers kept their eyes on the house. Occasionally I glanced at the wooden plank, thinking that at any moment the sniper would come rushing out with his gun blazing.

I glanced down the alley. A door opened. Steve flinched. Standing in the doorway was an old woman with her hair in curlers. She looked at us and then yelled something into the house. A moment later a middle-aged woman with red hair appeared at the door with her.

"Oh, he's got a camera," she said.

Then I realized they were looking at me. They had heard my American accent. Having British soldiers in their alley was no novelty, but an American photographer was something else. I smiled back at them nervously.

Timms came running down the alley. "Okay, men. We're going to go in." He was panting for breath.

A voice sounded from his radio. Timms answered, "Whiskey II to Delta. I'm going to enter the building from the rear."

Timms nodded to Steve, who stood to his feet bravely. There was a dangerous moment as the two soldiers climbed the wall. With cut glass and barbed wire, it was awkward to get a good grip. Finally they made it. The two soldiers darted across the wooden plank and disappeared into the house.

"I thought they weren't supposed to go in until they got help."

"They're already here," John mumbled. "Soldiers in the front."

We waited. I was worried. I thought about Corporal Timms and the private. I could see their bodies sprawled out on the floor of the house. I was overwhelmed by a feeling of disgust. No more terror now. Just a sick feeling in my stomach. *I hope nothing happens.*

Another patrol came running down the alley. A sergeant was leading. He was much younger than Corporal Timms. He seemed to be amused to find us leaning up against the wall. "Where are they?"

John explained the situation.

The sergeant looked at my tape recorder and camera. "*Time* magazine?" he asked.

"No. I'm a free-lance writer doing an article for *Christian Life.*"

John perked up. "You won't find any Christians over here."

The sergeant corrected him. "You'll find a lot of them, actually," he smiled.

"Really?"

"Yes. They're all hypocrites," he said. "They'll shoot you. An' then they go and confess it afterwards."

"Has anyone in your patrol ever been hit?"

"Couple of Fridays ago, one of my buddies was shot."

"Was he killed?"

"No," the sergeant hesitated. "He was lucky. It didn't hit anything of importance."

"Is he in the hospital?"

"No. He's in England."

"How long was he with you?"

"One day. His first day."

"I thought you said he was lucky. Where did they hit him?'

"His shoulder." The sergeant grabbed his shoulder, and I noticed his vest.

"Do all of you have these bulletproof vests?"

The sergeant looked at John. They both chuckled. "They're not bulletproof, actually."

"They're not?"

"The chap who invented them, he never had to wear them." We all laughed. "Actually it saved my buddy's life."

There were voices coming from the house. Timms and Steve raced across the plank and jumped down into the alley.

"Someone's been up there," Corporal Timms said.

"How did they get away?"

"Dunno. They may have come back across this plank before we got here. But someone's been up there. There's a big hole in the roof facin' that way and there's another facin' this way. He's built himself a little nest up there. There's a bench for him to stand on."

The sergeant looked suspiciously at the house *and* the corporal. "Well, it's a deterrent then." He and his men walked down the alley.

"Yeah."

"You report it?" the sergeant called back down the alley.

"Yeah!" The corporal watched the sergeant disappear.

"We'll move out this way, men. Let's get him to a taxi."

We walked the length of the alley and out onto Antrim Road."You see the taxi office over there?"

"Yes." I turned to the soldiers to thank them. "Well, I'll be in England next week."

They smiled. "Kiss the dirt for me," someone joked.

"How long have you been here?" I asked.

"Four weeks," Timms said. "But we've lived a lifetime. The first week we was here there was a riot on this block."

There was a break in the traffic on Antrim Road, so I raced across. I ordered a taxi and then walked out onto the sidewalk to watch the foot patrol disappear up a side street.

The sun had fallen behind a row of stone houses. *Probably only an hour of daylight left*, I thought. The traffic seemed to move a little faster and the people walked briskly. There was that feeling in the air that seems to happen every evening as people rush to their homes. In an hour the streets would be deserted. Belfast was preparing herself for another night.

*Somewhere in the neighborhood there's a man with a gun,* I thought. *I hope the patrol gets back.*

# 7

# The Antrim Road Murders

On Friday night, March 23, 1973, three British soldiers were machine-gunned to death by an IRA execution squad in a flat on Antrim Road.

Twenty-eight-year-old Sergeant Thomas Penrose telephoned his wife in Liverpool, England, that night. They talked about their six-year-old son, Ian. Penrose told her he was lonely and fed up with all the trouble.

"He told me he was going into the mess for a drink and would probably watch the telly," she told a reporter later.

Instead, Penrose was persuaded to join three other sergeants for a night in the city.

"We're gonna go to Pat and Jean's place," someone said.

Off-duty British soldiers cannot leave their base unless they are in groups of four. Penrose may have felt the pressure to make up a foursome. He was lonely and bored anyway. He decided to join the girls.

The sergeants had met Pat and Jean weeks before at the Woodlands Hotel in Lisburn. The Woodlands is a favorite off-duty spot of the British soldiers and only a mile from army headquarters, where I had spent the afternoon with Lieutenant Colonel Sillitoe.

Employees at the hotel were reluctant to talk to Steve Strang, one of our researchers (and a reporter for the *Orlando*

*Sentinel* in Florida). But after some persuasion one of them agreed to describe the girls as he remembered them. The girl known as Jean had dark, wavy hair with a small upturned nose. She was "well-built" and probably twenty years old. Her accomplice, Pat, was a slim blonde with long, shoulder-length hair. The girls were remembered as "smart dressers."

Thomas Penrose may have suspected something. The girls were beautiful and well-spoken. It could be a trap. He must have also considered the fact that he was the only Protestant along. The other three soldiers were Roman Catholic.

Shortly after he telephoned his wife in England, he checked out an army pistol. Penrose was a professional soldier with ten years' experience, but he was beginning to feel the pressure of the Irish conflict. He was nervous. When the girls actually arrived at the base, Penrose made a last-minute decision. He left his gun behind. Any apprehension about the evening vanished during the ride into the city.

Pat and Jean had arranged a party in their flat on Antrim Road, a so-called neutral part of Belfast. On his way into the second-floor room, Staff Sgt. Barrington Foster glanced down the road toward a military police base only a hundred yards away.

Pat and Jean had a fire burning in the hearth and food was already prepared. There was a dance or two before Pat slipped out, saying that she was going to bring back two of her girlfriends to join the party. All of the men were single except for Penrose, so the prospect of each with his own girl sounded exciting. Jean poured the drinks.

Moments later the door burst open. Pat had returned with two men. One was carrying a Thompson submachine gun and the other a pistol.

It had been a carefully planned trap. The apartment had been rented under an assumed name and had not been occupied because of a complaint that the electricity had not been connected. The beautiful girls had selected their victims weeks in advance. The party itself was a last-minute surprise, so the soldiers couldn't leave word where they were going. With spine-chilling efficiency the girls had lured their four new friends to the murder scene.

"Lay on the bed," the two gunmen ordered.

The helpless soldiers laid face down on the bed side by side. One by one, the machine gunner blasted short-range bursts through the head and body of each man. The bed splintered and cracked beneath the four soldiers. Their bodies twisted and shook as the bullets riddled them. Within seconds Jean, Pat, and the two assassins had disappeared into the night.

Staff Sergeant Foster and Michael Muldoon, a twenty-five-year-old sergeant from Northumberland, died within minutes. Thomas Penrose hung on to life until the next day. The fourth soldier dragged himself, bleeding, out of the second-floor room. He rolled down the stairs and crawled his way out of the building into the garden in front of the apartment.

Above the murder flat, a curious tenant began to hear groans coming from the hallway. She followed the trail of mysterious sounds down the stairway and into the room. There, lying in a pool of blood on the bed were three of the soldiers. The young woman could only scream hysterically again and again.

Across Antrim Road, Mr. Fred Curran nervously watched a young teen-age girl approach his store.

"There's a man who's been shot on the steps over there!"

Curran rushed across the street and found the soldier bleeding to death. He stood helpless for a moment and then ran back to his shop to call police.

Within thirty minutes military police had sealed off the area and top-ranking detectives had arrived at the scene. Forensic experts carefully examined the bodies while detectives questioned everyone in the building one by one. The young woman who had discovered the bodies remained hysterical and was rushed to a nearby hospital in a state of shock.

The massacre sent a wave of horror across the British Isles. Newspapers immediately reported that the IRA was responsible for the killings. An IRA source told reporters the soldiers were suspected of being a part of a British army spy ring. British officials denied that; they said the murders were a "coldly calculated operation."

"What the IRA apparently didn't know—or did not care about—was that three of the soldiers who were shot were themselves Catholic," a British officer explained, "And the fourth soldier was married to a Catholic."

Official response to killings was immediate. British Prime Minister Edward Heath told reporters that "the cowardly shooting of four more soldiers emphasizes that neither the duties nor the sacrifices of the security forces are yet at an end."

An RUC official said, "This particular murder sickens me to the pit of my stomach. These people must be caught. We have got used to some pretty horrifying crimes in the past three years—but this one is in a league of its own."

The grief-stricken father of one of the soldiers told the *Sunday Mirror,* "If I had my way, I would pull every British soldier out of that terrible country and then blow it out of the seas."

Mrs. Penrose was quoted in the *Daily Mirror* as saying, "I can't understand his murder. It's so senseless and unmerciful." She told reporters she was ashamed to be a Catholic.

Within hours of the killing, the Royal Ulster Constabulary formed a murder hunt headquarters at their Glen Ravel Street station. The surviving soldier, near death, gave important information in describing the girls who had lured him and his companions into the trap. The soldier's teeth and most of his jawbone had been shot away at point-blank range by bullets, yet he managed to communicate with muffled syllables.

A special machine, said to be the only one of its kind in the world, was installed at the Glen Ravel RUC station to receive information and descriptions of the two girls and present a photo likeness instantly.

By Sunday, thousands of large "Wanted" posters with the girls' pictures appeared across the British Isles. Helicopters carried quantities of the posters to inland villages and army bases in Northern Ireland.

The pictures also appeared on television and on the front pages of newspapers, with bold headlines describing the massacre.

Within two days the RUC station had received twenty-five hundred telephone calls offering information about the killing. They got descriptions of the two gunmen. Arrests seemed imminent. The most ambitious dragnet of the war had begun, involving thousands of police and soldiers.

On Tuesday, March 27, Mr. James McRoberts, Belfast's deputy coroner, held an inquest on the murdered soldiers. McRoberts, a Protestant, was a sensitive man who had resigned as town solicitor in Londonderry because of the discrimination against Catholics.

The same day, he held an inquest into the death of a youth killed by a sniper and a lorry driver shot in the chest. In fact, before the day was over McRoberts had investigated six violent deaths.

His closing remarks at the inquest for the soldiers revealed the extent of his personal anguish. "It is sad that these young men should have died while trying to help us sort out our own problems."

McRoberts joined his wife Marjorie for a night out together. Later in the evening they returned to their home in Bangor, County Down. He left the room for a cup of tea.

Marjorie found his body in the garage. The fifty-two-year-old deputy coroner had hung himself. His friends believe that he could no longer face the hatred and suffering of a divided Northern Ireland.

By Wednesday, it was apparent that the greatest manhunt in the British Isles had been an embarrassing failure. The IRA execution squad had vanished into thin air.

Police concluded that the killers were being protected by the Catholic community, a very likely probability. Many of the "Wanted" posters displaying the girls' pictures were torn down in the Catholic ghettos. One poster, only yards from the murder flat, was ripped down seconds after troops had pinned it to a telegraph pole. In London, Catholic civil rights leader Bernadette Devlin and actress Vanessa Redgrave publicly announced an offer of refuge and accommodations for ten Irish Catholics accused at the time of bombings there.

"I've had experiences with British soldiers," said a Catholic customs official, Mr. Costigan. "When I hear of them being killed, I just think 'Well, that's their hard luck!' I have no sympathy for them!"

The British soldiers arrived in 1971. They were considered

saviors of the Catholic people. Against a background of growing violence and rioting, the Westminster government had suspended the Northern Ireland Constitution and removed Brian Faulkner as prime minister. William Whitelaw, an Englishman, was appointed secretary of state for the province, and Britain assumed direct rule. One of Whitelaw's first decisions was to end the unpopular internment policy of suspected terrorists.

But within weeks, the ancient Irish hatred of the English resurfaced. Ninety-eight soldiers died the first year while trying to contain a spreading violence that caused more than three hundred civilian deaths. Before the end of 1973, the death total from terrorist assassinations and bombings climbed to nine hundred.

Every morning, the BBC's Northern Ireland newscast (which is not heard in Britain itself) begins with an overnight report of the casualties. The broadcast is a frightening recitation of shootings, bombings, and killings. The newscast ends, however, with the list of local events—choral-society meetings, agricultural competitions, sports—which proves that some normal life does go on, even in the middle of the violence.

For many people in Northern Ireland, life can never be normal again. Things will never be normal for the young wife whose husband, a part-time soldier, was shot in the head while he delivered milk on a lonely country road forty-three miles southwest of Belfast. Nor will life be normal for the twelve-year-old lad who lost an eye after being hit with a rubber bullet from a British soldier's anti-riot gun. Nor will it be normal for the young Catholic girl who was maimed on the eve of her wedding when the IRA bombed a restaurant she was in. Dublin's *Irish Times* complained about the incident: "Two legs gone, one arm sheared off, an eye lost, all in one female body. That equals someone's idea of patriotism in Ireland in 1972."

Because of the violence, both the Protestant and Catholic communities have completed the process of polarization. A large population shift in Belfast has taken place in the last two years. *Time* magazine reported that in 1971, about twenty-five percent of the people in public housing projects lived in mixed areas; today virtually none do. More than ten thousand families have moved since 1969, five thousand within the year 1973 alone; about eighty percent are Catholics who have moved to West Belfast, which is fast becoming the city's single, sprawling Catholic ghetto.

After eight centuries, the tortured war is still not resolved.

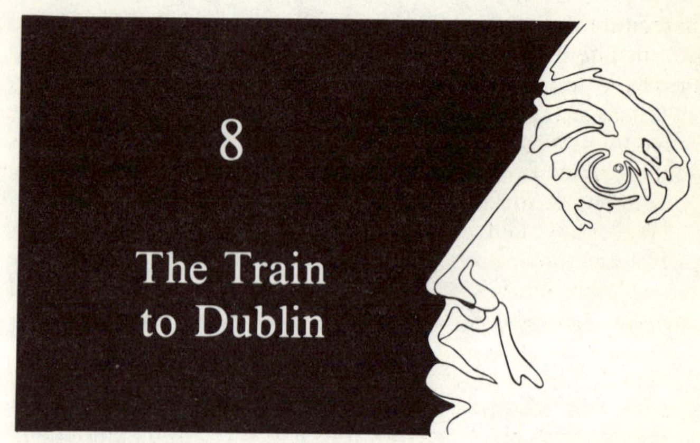

# 8 The Train to Dublin

You can learn a lot about Irish history by riding the train to Dublin. All the books and magazines I had devoured in the last year didn't make the same kind of impression.

It is a beautiful ride. You wind through rolling, green farmlands dotted by some houses and churches. You pass through Drogheda, sight of the Cromwell massacre. Then you cross the River Boyne, where William of Orange defeated King James II and the Catholics.

It's impossible to understand the crisis in Ulster today without considering the whole history of Ireland, but that's a problem. A lot of books have been written—most of them so boring that only the Irish and English read them. The story is so complex that some of the most concrete facts are occasionally challenged.

On the train to Dublin, I found two self-proclaimed history experts. One was a Catholic, the other a Protestant. Occasionally they got their dates and personalities mixed up. Their interpretation of history was at times debatable. But the important thing is they believe it is true. What the Irish think happened is almost as important as what really did.

I met Mr. Thomas McEwen in the dining car. I hadn't eaten a meal on a train since I was nine years old, so I decided to enjoy the clean, starched tablecloth with beautiful, heavy silverware. I was seated opposite Thomas at a table for four. I dumped my Air New Zealand flight bag in the empty chair next to me.

"I'm Doug Wead, American press."

His mouth was full, but he managed to smile. "Thomas McEwen," he finally said.

"You going to Dublin to visit?"

"Well, I have no friends there," he said. "It's a business trip."

Thomas took another mouthful of peas. I looked out of the large glass window as beautiful scenes raced by. *This is great,* I thought. *I hope Amtrak makes it.*

"You're covering the trouble, I suppose?" he asked.

"Yes." Which reminded me to stop daydreaming. I pulled out my tape recorder. "Do you mind if I interview you?"

He looked at me with a mixture of curiosity and amusement. "Sure. I don't know what I could tell you, though."

"Have you been involved in the violence in any way?"

"No." But he immediately corrected himself. "Well, I've had friends." He was staring out the window, chewing on a piece of tough steak, and trying to think of something that might interest an American journalist.

I took advantage of the silence to give my order to the waiter.

"My parents' house blew one night," he said.

"Are you Protestant or Catholic?"

"Catholic." The train shook and rattled as we sped around a corner.

"Okay, what happened?"

"Well, my parents live in this tiny little village and their home is right next to the constabulary office."

"The police?"

"Yes. Someone had planted a bomb in the office. When it blew, it destroyed their house with it."

"Were they home?"

"Luckily not. They were not injured at all. Of course, they lost everything."

"Do you approve of this violence?"

Mr. McEwen winced. "Well, I want a united Ireland. I think every true Irishman wants that."

"Northern Ireland just voted overwhelmingly to stay in the

United Kingdom," I said. "They rejected union with the Irish Republic *and* a united Ireland."

"Well," Thomas smiled and looked at my tape recorder in exasperation. "Do you know anything about Irish history?"

"Give me a quick review."

He laughed.

"I have a research team helping me," I said, smiling. "We've been poring through documents and books this past year."

His amusement gave way to a more serious look. "Then you've read about Pope Adrian IV?"

I nodded; that was a good place to start discussing Irish history. In 1154, Pope Adrian IV gave Ireland as an inheritance to King Henry II of England. The English promptly invaded to claim their new land. Ireland at the time was only a loose confederation, but the kings united to resist the intruder. The wars for control of Ireland lasted for generations, the Irish fighting for freedom, the English claiming control.

"What is most important to remember is that Pope Adrian was himself an Englishman—the only English pope in history." Thomas looked at me to see if I understood the significance. "Thank God there hasn't been another English pope," he added.

"Why do the Irish hate the British so?"

He was in the process of buttering a roll, but he dropped his knife at that question. "Five centuries!" he said angrily. "For five centuries the English armies tried to conquer us! They ruined our farmlands, raped our women, killed our sons! Five centuries!" He stared out the window in a daze, and then returned quickly to announce, "That's fifteen generations. Well, each generation had a good reason to hate the British. That just can't be easily forgotten."

"When did the English finally conquer Ireland?"

"Under Queen Elizabeth." He couldn't remember the date. (It was 1601.) "They tried to make everyone Protestants," he said. "When they couldn't succeed, they drove the Irish earls off the land and brought over Protestant Scots and Englishmen. The Protestants got the land, and the Catholics worked as cheap labor."

"So the Protestants who live in Ulster today are the descendants of the Scottish and Englishmen who came over to rule the Catholics and to pacify Ireland?"

"That's right!" His food was now cold, so he pushed his plate away.

"Were there any uprisings during this time?"

"Oh yes, every generation. There was fighting all over the country. You've heard of Oliver Cromwell?"

"Yes."

"Well, he beheaded the king of England for suspected Catholicism! Then he took over and became a dictator. He came to Ireland and burned city after city!"

"The Drogheda massacre?"

"Yes. Well, we will pass through Drogheda in a few minutes." He looked at his watch.

"How many Catholics died at Drogheda?"

"More than four thousand, I think." He was right. In 1638, Cromwell's campaign began. He brought over more English settlers to help control the Irish. By 1660, Catholics, who outnumbered the Protestants ten to one, only owned one-seventh of the land.

The train rolled into a city.

"Drogheda," Thomas said. It's a city of about twenty thousand people, old gray buildings, churches, and stone houses. My meal arrived, so our conversation ended for a few minutes. Then the Irish Sea came into view. It was beautiful from the train. There was a long sandy beach. We rumbled across a bridge. Beneath us a wide river flowed into the sea.

"The Boyne River?"

"Yes."

"You mean the Battle of the Boyne was fought here?" I didn't expect it to be in Drogheda.

Thomas smiled. "You know all about that, I suppose."

Perhaps no other event in Irish history is as famous as the Battle of the Boyne. After Oliver Cromwell, the Stuarts came to power. One of the English kings, James II, was a secret Catholic. When his conversion to Catholicism was discovered, he was deposed and Prince William of Orange took the crown of England.

In 1689, James II landed in Ireland. He organized the Irish

Catholics into a great army in an attempt to retake the throne. First, he overran the Protestant landlords in Ireland. Thirty thousand Protestant Ulstermen retreated to Derry. The Catholic army surrounded them. The siege lasted 105 days, but the Protestants held. That event is celebrated annually by the Protestants of the city, which has since been renamed Londonderry.

One year later, William of Orange landed with the English army. James II met him at the Boyne River July 1, 1690. It was the critical moment in a long struggle between Catholic and Protestant interests. On the English side, King William III, Prince of Orange, a staunch Dutch Protestant. On the Catholic side, James II with his Irish army. The Irish Catholics were defeated decisively.

"What happened after the Battle of the Boyne?"

"The English ruled—that's what happened! You see, this is more than Catholic against Protestant. During the 1700s, even the Protestants wanted freedom from England."

"Wolfe Tone?"

"Yes. He was a Protestant, but he believed in a free Ireland. The IRA and all of the nationalist groups identify with him."

"When did the IRA begin?"

Thomas smiled. "First, there were the Fenians."

The Fenians were nationalists who used bombs and assassination to demonstrate against British presence in the 1800s. Their romantic adventures captured the imagination of Irish youth for more than a century and provided temporary victories for the intimidated Catholics. By 1905, the Fenians had reorganized into a political party called the Sinn Fein (Ourselves Alone). The famed Irish Republican Army was begun eight years later.

"Let's talk about the Easter Rebellion."

The conductor interrupted our conversation. I couldn't find my ticket. My hands went from pocket to pocket until I finally found the little yellow rectangle.

"That was our Declaration of Independence," Thomas said.

On Easter Monday 1916, Patrick Pearse stood in front of the Dublin General Post Office and read his proclamation. The rebellion began. The British army was taken by surprise. Important government buildings were occupied; and before the day was over, the rebels controlled the center of the city.

The British struck back. There was a week of bloody combat in Dublin before the rebels surrendered. Fifteen leaders were executed, including poet Patrick Pearse and the Socialist Labor leader James Connally. Four thousand were arrested.

Many Irish Catholics had not supported the violence of the Fenians and the IRA, but they were horrified by the executions and arrests that followed the Easter Rebellion. Now the nationalist movement had martyrs. Revolution spread across Ireland.

"Did the Irish have any freedom or self-government during these years?"

"No!" Thomas was angry.

As a matter of fact, the British Parliament did decide to give Ireland home rule in 1914. However, these plans were postponed by Protestant pressures from Ulster and the advent of World War I.

"When did Ireland get her freedom?"

"She never has completely," Mr. McEwen said impatiently. "In 1918, the British asked the Irish to vote. They overwhelmingly, by more than eighty percent, voted for a united, free Ireland. But Britain wouldn't give it to her. Even now, Northern Ireland is a part of the United Kingdom."

"But the Irish Republic is a sovereign, Catholic nation, with its capital in Dublin. It's free, isn't it?"

"Yes, but Ireland is not united. How did you feel when the South said she wanted to pull away from the United States and run her own country? You fought a civil war; the majority ruled. But England didn't let us organize our own country; she divided us up."

"When did this partition take place?"

"1921."

After the Easter Rebellion, there were five years of bloody fighting. Prime Minister Lloyd George of England signed a treaty with the revolutionaries. The Irish Republic was born. There are thirty-eight counties in Ireland. Thirty-two voted to join the new republic. The six counties of Ulster voted to stay with the British.

"Shouldn't Northern Ireland have the right to decide for themselves whether they want to join the Irish Republic?"

"If you'd have had the South vote during the Civil War, they would've wanted to separate, too. But a country should not keep splitting up. You didn't allow it."

I looked out the window. The sun was setting. We were in the countryside again. An old man was peddling a bicycle down a narrow road. A woman was hanging clothes on her line. The beautiful panorama of rolling hills passed by.

Mr. McEwen picked up his newspaper in the seat next to him and started to get up.

"Oh, thanks so much for the interview." I turned off my tape recorder.

Thomas smiled shyly. "Well, good luck to you."

I repacked my flight bag and left the dining room through the opposite door.

My search for a Protestant historian was awkward. Most of the people riding the train into Dublin were Catholics. I did finally talk to a teen-ager.

"I'm a Presbyterian," he said.

"Do you know anything about Oliver Cromwell?"

"Does he live in Belfast?" he asked.

I cut that interview very short.

Eventually I found Mr. and Mrs. Harold Lindley. They were all wrapped up in their coats, seated by themselves in the last car. They were quite nervous as I approached them.

When I started asking questions, Mrs. Lindley got angry. She stared straight ahead. Harold had a great big plastic smile on his face that hardly varied for the next hour. His cheeks were flushed, and I was afraid that at any moment he would tell me to move on. I was sure they were Protestants.

"Look, I'm an American writer. All I want to do is ask you some questions about Irish history."

Harold was curious. "What do you want to know?"

I told him about Thomas McEwen.

"Well, it seems that you ought to give the Protestants equal time." His big stomach shook with laughter beneath his coat, but his eyes were very serious. The way he said *Protestants* intrigued me. It was almost under his breath, so that no one heard it but me.

"You talked about Oliver Cromwell, I suppose?" he asked.

I nodded.

"Well, did you ever consider that there was some reason why Cromwell had to come over here?" Once again his stomach jiggled.

"Revolution," I said.

"No. The settlers from England were being slaughtered." Now his face was serious. "Irish clans were burning homes, killing entire families." He paused. "Did you know that it was a pope who urged England to annex Ireland in the first place?"

"He was an English pope, Adrian IV," I said.

Mr. Lindley looked at me with surprise. "He wasn't English!"

"I'm serious; he really was," I said politely.

"Well, it doesn't matter. The pope's infallible anyway, isn't he?" I thought Harold was going to roll out of his seat with laughter. Even Mrs. Lindley smiled.

"What do you think of Ian Paisley?" I asked.

Mrs. Lindley lit up. "Oh, he's a great preacher, a great preacher! Have you ever heard him?"

"No."

Harold's face looked disturbed. He touched his wife on the knee to signal that she was too loud. I noticed a man nearby. His eyes darted from his newspaper when he heard me mention Paisley.

Harold leaned in to me and whispered, "The IRA is murderous. When the Catholics got their nation, the first president of the Irish Republic was a commander of the Easter Rebellion."

"DeValera?" I interrupted.

"Yes, DeValera. But when he became president, he arrested leaders in the IRA, his old friends."

"Why?"

"Because they're murderers. You can't run a government with them."

"They're communists!" Mrs. Lindley said loudly. Harold squeezed her knee tightly, then looked around the train car smiling to see who heard her.

"It is no secret that they get their arms from the Russians," Harold whispered.

The accusations sounded unbelievable, coming from such comical personalities. (But the next day, the Irish navy captured the ship *Claudia*. On board was Joe Cahill, leader of the Belfast Provisional IRA. With him were five tons of weapons and ammunitions, including 250 Russian-made rifles and 20,000 rounds of Russian-made ammunition.)

"What's the solution?" I asked.

"If the British would leave Northern Ireland, our boys could clean up the mess in two months."

"Now, who do you mean? Do you mean the Protestant government?"

"Yes, the Royal Ulster Constabulary. Other groups would help."

"The B Specials?" I was asking him about a special organization of men whom the Protestant government first put into uniforms in the 1920s. To Roman Catholics, the B Specials were dreaded like Hitler's SA. They operated until the British persuaded the Ulster government to disband them. Most of them have quietly enrolled in militant Protestant organizations such as the UDA.

He smiled. "Sure, they could do it by themselves." And he laughed some more.

"Do you belong to the Orange Order?"

Harold glanced around, then shook his head. "Oh, I couldn't tell you that."

"That's against the rules, huh?"

His eyes twinkled. "Well, it's a secret organization. Sir Winston's father, Lord Randolph Churchill, was a member."

The Orange Society began in 1795, more than a century after the Battle of the Boyne was fought. Protestants of Ulster organized the Orange Society in memory of "the pious and immortal King William III" (William of Orange), who defeated the Catholics.

To this day, the Orangemen still celebrate the Battle of the Boyne in a huge parade. In 1969, rioting followed after one of these demonstrations. Some refer to that moment as the beginning of the current crises.

It was dark outside. The train rumbled through a suburb of Dublin. I decided that I'd better return to my baggage.

"Will Ireland ever unite?" I asked.

"Not without a war, she won't." Harold gritted his teeth.

I picked up my tape recorder, which had been lying on the seat in front of them. Harold looked at his wife and then stared back at my recorder as if he had been betrayed. "What's that?"

"A tape recorder." I tried to explain why I needed it, but it only made Mrs. Lindley more angry.

The man across the aisle put down his newspaper and squinted at me suspiciously.

"Good luck!" I smiled, ignoring their reaction to my tape recorder. They didn't answer. Mrs. Lindley mumbled angrily in her husband's ear. Harold just sat there, red in the face.

It wouldn't have helped to do any more explaining, so I left them to their fears. I started working my way back to the right compartment.

*What's going to happen to Ireland now?* I thought to myself. *Is there any chance for peace? Must this violence and misery be passed on to yet another generation?*

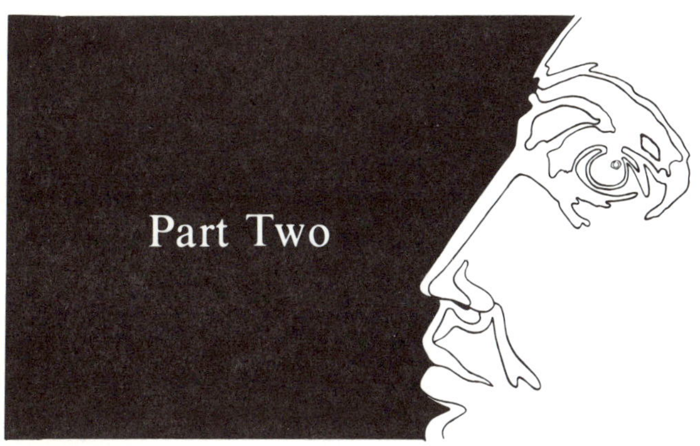


*A cool wind rushes across Dundrum Bay and into the rocky coast. It ascends Slieve Donard Mountain almost three thousand feet up into the fog. It rides the waters of the Lagan River, falling down through rugged woodlands and past green meadows. Down, down the wind sweeps, blowing into the cities where it whips through narrow streets, pushing the pollution before it out into the sea. It is not just industrial pollution that meets this wind in the cities. It is the pollution of men's hearts. It is the accumulation of eight centuries of division and hatred. The children choke in it. The parents have breathed it all their lives and do nothing about it. This is Northern Ireland, a land of violence and murder, and this is the story of the courageous young Irish who have welcomed that new wind.*

# 9
# There's a Prayer Meeting at Queen's University

Approximately seventy young people were sitting in chairs, piled on a sofa, leaning against the wall, but mostly sprawled over the floor. It was so crowded that when I entered there was a ripple of laughter as everyone readjusted to make room for one more.

The Queen's University surroundings were old. Three lamps hung from a place where there had once been a chandelier. The carpeting was new but the design was quaint. Brown drapes covered the windows. A book rack displayed the works of C. S. Lewis and other Christian writers.

The speaker was giving a rather crisp warning that this Jesus movement involved more than experiences; "it means obedience to the Word of God."

When he finished, there was a moment of silence. Then a large girl, quite self-conscious, managed to say, "I want to sing."

She began awkwardly: "Jesus is the Way, the Truth, and the Life." But before she said the word *Life* dozens of voices had joined hers.

One young man, long-haired and bearded, smiled dreamily at the ceiling throughout the entire session. A girl in a red sweater sat quietly with her eyes shut. There was a strum of a guitar and everyone began to sing joyously.

Let there be peace in our land,
Let there be peace in our people,
Let there be peace in our lives,
from now on.

For a moment we seemed to forget where we were. But when the last note died, it was again very quiet. A broken, helpless feeling returned.

It was ten-thirty. We didn't know it, but at that moment a member of the Royal Ulster Constabulary lay dying in a ditch three miles outside the Belfast city limits. A dozen bullets had been pumped into his stomach.

In the corner a girl began to weep softly. From the other side of the room came a young man's voice.

"We pray, Father, help us to intercede for this country. Teach us how to intercede for our leaders, for people who use violence. We pray, Father, that You will give us the grace to take up the cross that we need to take up here, for Jesus' sake."

There was no amen. He just stopped. At that point something seemed to happen to everyone. One would have thought Jesus Himself had entered the room. The young lady in the red sweater prayed.

"We love You because You first loved us. We pray that many others will find this love. We pray that You will bring this love to our city . . . and to 'Derry, and to all who are in fear." She paused a long time. Then with great force she concluded, "Father, by Thy Spirit's power give us now an understanding of love."

Tony prayed, too. Tony is a young man who works in a bar. He talks to people about Christianity and about love. Sometimes his comments are unwelcome. "Thank you for the courage of those who have suffered and still come back," he said.

At that moment I realized how unpopular this movement might be.

"We pray for all who are afraid." I turned to see the Reverend Cecil Kerr, chaplain at Queen's. He was reverent and quiet, yet his face betrayed a curious frustration and agony. "We pray for all who are threatened. We pray for hearts that are filled with hate." He hesitated and swallowed. "We ask that Your love will break their hearts of hate. May Your name be glorified by all that we do."

I slipped out of the building and into the cold night air, a bit confused by what I had seen. Religion is partly responsible for the Irish trauma; it hardly seems likely that religion would also be an answer.

Yet I was impressed. I had spent a full day visiting various unity groups. Most of them were old women's tea parties. They would generate some publicity by calling for Catholics and Protestants to quit fighting. The women's groups would grow for a few months and then fail for lack of interest. At Queen's University the group was clearly different. They were religious, yet interdenominational. There were similar prayer groups throughout the city involving Catholics, Baptists, Lutherans, Presbyterians, and the Church of Ireland. And they involved great numbers of young people.

Eventually I arranged to meet the founder of the first charismatic prayer group in Northern Ireland. He was a mild, soft-spoken Catholic businessman, Frank Forte.

"It started with Pope John when he said to open the windows," Frank gestured as though he were reaching for the right word. "Dialogue," he announced. "And that meant meeting people, of course. So, I met people—Presbyterians, Methodists, Pentecostals—but I had the wrong slant of dialogue."

"When was this?" I asked.

"About four years ago."

"Go on."

"Well, I did a lot of talking with a friend at work. He was a Pentecostal. But we used the Scriptures as daggers against each other. Once we ended up in an argument. Then one day I wrote a priest friend about this Pentecostalism. He answered me and said that there was now teaching in the church (Catholic) about this, but to go easy. So, I returned to the Scriptures, and I no longer argued with my friend. We discussed different ideas, and I began to read."

What Frank Forte read was that the Pentecostal movement or charismatic renewal was an interdenominational force involving millions of people throughout the world.

Ireland had its traditional Pentecostals, of course, who traced their beginnings to the early 1900s and had formed their own churches and denominations. There were also the neo-Pentecostals, like the Baptist pastor who claimed to have the gift of speaking in tongues (a mysterious New Testament gift which allows one to pray in another language without actually having learned it).

But on January 10, 1971, a Catholic prayer group began at the Kimmage Manor in Dublin. It started with a group of religious students who were frustrated by the Irish problem. They had considered Christian socialism and even revolutionary action. Finally through a series of mysterious circumstances, they came to believe that the solution lay somewhere in the powerful charismatic movement which was beginning to sweep the world. It seemed to have a healing power and an ecumenicity that was needed in Ireland.

After the beginnings at Kimmage Manor, Frank Forte was assured that his activities were not un-Catholic. Two months later he began to meet with his Protestant friend for prayer. They prayed for peace. They prayed for renewal. The movement came to Belfast. Within two years there were dozens of prayer groups all over Ulster, and students of the university were meeting for prayer during the lunch hours.

One common denominator united them all, a faith in Jesus Christ. The Protestants usually referred to a moment of "salvation" or "experiencing Christ as your personal Savior." The Catholics referred to the same experience as a "realization of baptism." Both agreed that something unusual was happening to thousands across Ireland.

# 10
# A Revolution of Love

A thousand miles to the southeast, the Italian mountains rose high above the Adriatic Sea. Patrick Murphy coasted his scooter down the winding road toward Trieste. The golden sun shined brilliantly above him.

He shifted gears, and the scooter lurched forward. Pat's girlfriend, Carol, held on tighter and squealed with delight. The wind whipped their tanned faces, and her hair streamed behind her. Faster and faster they raced, until the trees and rocks were only a blur.

*Wish this summer could last forever,* he thought to himself. Then the depressing sensation of Northern Ireland bore down on him. Only a few days left, and his summer on the continent would come to an end. He would have to go back. Anyway, the revolution needed him. Sometimes he got tired of working and tired of politics, but a good socialist must do his duty.

*We have history on our side,* he contented himself. *Someday Ireland will be socialist and the fighting will be over. It may not happen in my lifetime, but it is inevitable.*

His scooter popped and hissed. Seconds later the engine died. "Oh, no," Pat groaned. He coasted the heavy machine to the bottom of the hill, then rolled off the side of the road.

A look in the gas tank and a couple of tries to start the machine convinced him that something was seriously wrong.

He sat down on the grass and looked out to the sea.

"What will we do now?" Carol said, and then she looked out to the horizon. "Isn't it beautiful?"

"Maybe we'll just stay here," he laughed. But inside, his day was turning into depressing shades of gray. *Where will I get the scooter fixed?* he wondered. *Maybe we should hitchhike.*

Pat could hear the sounds of a fishing village far below. The sun was like a warm blanket and he was tired.

"Hey, Pat! There's a house across the road. Maybe someone will help us."

He shook himself. "Yeah, I better do something while it's daylight." So they walked across the road.

An old woman greeted them at the door. She was all smiles.

"Do you speak English?" they asked her.

She didn't. But she could see they were stranded.

"*Parlez vous Francais?*" Pat asked.

The old woman answered back with enthusiasm.

Carol felt a little left out as the two tested each other's French. Both Pat and the old woman were fluent.

The old woman wouldn't do anything until she was sure that her guests had plenty to eat and felt comfortable.

"She wants you to take a shower and relax," Pat explained to his girlfriend.

Carol's eyes got big. A shower had become something of a luxury to the two summer vagabonds. Pat nodded, so she darted up the stairs.

Meanwhile, the old woman spread the table for Pat. The more he ate, the more she found to feed him until he was hopelessly behind and the table was still covered with food.

"Why don't you stay here?" she asked. She read his face and without another word prepared the beds.

Pat and Carol stayed several days. Their hostess even purchased special farewell gifts when they had to leave.

The old woman did talk a lot about Christianity, but Pat didn't mind. Everything she said he had heard before. Anyway, she wasn't trying to change him. She was genuinely humbled by the teachings of Christ, and she was quite thrilled about the chance she was having to help someone.

Pat Murphy had heard enough about religion. As a young

Methodist in Northern Ireland it was always "The wages of sin is death." Though he had not completely exhausted the possibilities of Christianity from an intellectual standpoint, he had other reasons to abandon it. The hatred and bitterness that permeates the air in Christian Ulster was sufficient evidence to him that faith in Christ alone was not the answer.

Yet he felt himself being drawn into conversation with the old woman. He didn't argue—after all, he was eating her food. Anyway, she was quite convincing. It wasn't what she actually said as much as the authenticity of her faith.

Pat Murphy was beginning to see that this seventy-year-old woman whom he had only met that day really cared about him. You just don't see that in Northern Ireland.

He told her about Belfast and the hatred and violence. She sobbed as they talked about the troubles.

"Maybe we should pray about it," the old woman finally said.

Pat bowed his head reverently. He couldn't explain it, but in that moment he really believed that there was a God who was listening to them. He couldn't have doubted it if he had tried. There seemed to be a suggestive power that emanated from the frail, old woman. The faith was stronger than anything Pat had ever encountered. "Perhaps it is emotion," he thought. It certainly wasn't anything she had said. For the moment he would just have to believe that there is a God somewhere.

Pat shook himself free and walked out of the house toward the mountain road. The sun was dropping right into the sea, sending myriads of brilliant colors across the waters and the sky. The sight momentarily overwhelmed him.

The thought of God was very much on his mind. God was no longer the remote possibility He seemed to be in an intellectual discussion with his friends. At that moment God was very strong and magnificent in His creation, and was very dramatic through the life of a tender old woman.

Pat laughed to himself as he thought of how naive and trusting she was. Then he felt selfish and guilty and very small.

There was a moment of anticipation—*Something is going to happen,* he thought. A blast of wind seemed to break loose from somewhere in the universe and come hurtling toward him at thousands of miles an hour until it became a great current of cold, refreshing wind, blowing some of the heat of the day before it.

*God loves me,* Pat realized at that moment. The wind rushed by him as though God were tenderly touching his cheek. *God loves me!*

Who can interpret spiritual experiences? Who can explain what actually takes place in a moment like that? If it were not for the dynamic change which occurred immediately in his life, Pat Murphy would have quickly forgotten the kind old woman who had touched his life with love.

Something had happened to him in northern Italy. Something so strong it would weather the pressures of Ireland. "I saw Christ through the life of that old Catholic woman," Pat said later.

For a while Pat was very much alone back at Queen's University in Belfast that fall. The Christians he met did not understand him. "The Catholics seemed to have great loyalty to their church," he concluded, "but no loyalty toward God. The Protestants kept insisting that all the Catholics would have to convert to Protestantism if there is to be salvation for Ulster."

Though he didn't doubt his own mission to bring some love back to Northern Ireland, he wondered why God hadn't impressed anyone else in Belfast in a similar way. He asked God for a friend.

Within days, he was told about a weekly meeting at the Church of Ireland campus center. He decided to check it out.

From the very first meeting, Pat Murphy realized that he was only part of a great spiritual revolution God was bringing to Ulster. He met dozens of other young people from all Protestant denominations who in their own way had been touched by God. A few days later he learned that there were similar Catholic prayer groups in the city. This love, this Christ ideal he had seen in the old Italian woman was portrayed through the lives of dozens of other Irish young people. He was overjoyed.

One of his first friends at the center was Marlene, a beautiful coed who had been reading about the charismatic renewal but was surprised to find it happening on her own campus.

Marlene had always felt that something was missing in her life. Her parents had no religious background at all, but they dutifully took their family once a year to the nearby Presbyterian church.

As Marlene grew older, she visited the church more often. At moments, she felt close to God, but that sensation always faded.

Sometimes she visited an elderly woman who had been neglected by her family. "I always came away feeling that I was glad I went and had a chat with her," she remembers. "She felt good when I visited her. I wanted to make other people happy, to enjoy life, and I found that I was able to do this."

Like Pat, she was very hungry for love. Several young men were eager to have her, but she was not yet convinced that physical love alone would be that meaningful.

One night, Marlene had a spiritual experience that changed her life. "I never realized until that night how much Christ really loved me. Not just part of me, but all of me. This is neat, because no one has ever loved me this much."

The meetings at the Church of Ireland center provided Pat and Marlene and dozens of other students with an explanation of what had happened to them.

Pat began to read his Bible long hours into the night. Soon his mysterious experience in northern Italy had a rational and theological explanation. Like others at the center, he referred to it as his "born-again" experience. Pat found himself using Scriptures and terms he had heard in his own Methodist church as a youth. Only "now it was different. Now the Scriptures seemed to be alive. Now they meant something. They worked!"

While the small movement which began at Queen's did in fact teach the same basic doctrines taught by mainstream Protestant Christianity, there were some important differences. The Queen's movement placed a greater emphasis on Christian living rather than spending long hours defining doctrine. They were practicing Christian methods and finding their actions far more powerful than handing out religious papers or preaching sermons to people.

Perhaps the most practical difference between traditional Protestantism and the new movement was the charismatic emphasis. This accounted for the attractive optimism and hope one could sense within the prayer groups. No one else really expected peace. It would take a miracle. But that was no problem for members of the charismatic prayer groups. They believed in miracles.

# 11

# New Hope for Ireland

The maid knocked on the door. I sat up in bed in an instant. She entered with a tray of hot tea and biscuits.

"Breakfast, sir," she said in a high-pitched voice, too cheerful for eight o'clock in the morning.

I waited until I heard the door shut behind her, then I sprang from the bed. After a long stretch, I pulled open the drapes. My eyes closed tightly as the bright sunshine poured into the room.

The tenth floor of the Europa Hotel has a magnificent view of Belfast. I glanced around the city every morning, and before retiring in the evening I repeated the ritual. That wall of glass provided scenes more exciting than television.

Something was going on this morning. Great Victoria Street, directly beneath me, was deserted. I glanced down to the corner. The RUC had roadblocks up. They were stopping all traffic. My eyes searched up and down the streets throughout the city center. Everything was normal and busy except on my street.

Then people started coming out of their shops and businesses. A few of them stood and looked in curiosity toward the railroad station next to the hotel. Hundreds were moving toward safety on the other side of the roadblocks. Some were walking fast, but most of them were running. Occasionally they would glance back over their shoulders to the center of attention. The scene reminded me of newsreels taken during the Hungarian revolution. In only moments a full block on Great Victoria Street had been emptied.

I opened the sliding window and leaned out as far as I could. It was a cold morning, and the tenth floor breeze made it colder. Whatever they were afraid of, it was out of my range. I couldn't see anything.

I left the window momentarily to fix my tea. I returned in time to see two British patrols converging on the scene. Another military mobile unit wound up a narrow street toward the hotel. Within five minutes the street was covered with dozens of heavy army vehicles, and even more police were arriving.

Directly beneath me a man in a suit darted out of the hotel lobby. He raced across the street and slowed down only as he reached the roadblock.

*Hmmm. Maybe it's the hotel,* I thought, sipping my hot tea.

The crowd on the other side of the roadblock swelled with hundreds of curious people, photographers and newsmen. A few were allowed to enter the sealed-off area. Occasionally someone would race into the area, start his parked car, and drive it away from the danger.

I had appointments at Queen's University that day, so after glancing at my watch I decided I should hurry.

In between shaving and getting dressed, I returned to the window to watch the dramatic developments on the street below. Another army patrol had arrived. I could tell by the vehicles that it was a demolition crew.

*It's a bomb!* I grabbed my Air New Zealand flight bag and raced to the elevator. The bomb had been planted in the Donaldson and Lyttle's furniture store on the corner of Great Victoria Street.

"It was supposed to have gone off fifteen minutes ago," a photographer said in disgust. He blew on his frozen fingers.

"Well, nothing's on time these days," someone commented in typical Irish black humor.

I waited with a cocked camera for thirty minutes in the cold before giving up and calling to a nearby taxi.

"How long will it take you to get me to Queen's University?"

"Not long, get in."

I first checked to see if he had a meter, then took one more look at the furniture store, which was still intact.

"Normally I could have you there in five minutes," he said, "but not when there's a bomb." The taxi followed a thick stream of traffic down a narrow street.

"Things were really bad last night," he continued without any encouragement. I turned on my tape recorder. "They were bombin' all over. There's nothin' nobody can do about it, either. Ya know the elections they had? Only two percent voted what the IRA told 'em to. They ain't very many of 'em, but they sure mess things up, they do."

I wondered about the charismatic movement. It's not very big, either—but perhaps it will succeed out of proportion to its numbers.

I had talked about it with a group of newsmen in the lounge at the hotel. Jerry King of ABC was especially interested.

"I didn't know anything like that was going on."

"I don't think the British can solve it," someone added.

After eating lunch at the university with Rev. Kerr, he welcomed me into his office. His desk was filled with piles of papers and books. Outside a window, a chimney pumped ugly black smoke into the sky.

"Billy Graham visited here, didn't he?" I asked.

"Yes," Kerr answered. "He spoke at the Social Science Lecture Theater to five or six hundred. It was during final exams, so that is a good attendance."

"Did you hear him?"

"Yes, actually I introduced him. It was a very exciting moment for me. I remember he changed his subject that morning. He spoke on a 'revolution of love.' The students were spellbound."

"Did the Catholics participate in the service?"

Rev. Kerr smiled and nodded. "Billy Graham had said that he would come only if all of the chaplains invited him. So we did. The Catholic chaplain closed the meeting."

I shifted in my chair and pulled my notebook from my bag. "How did this campus Jesus movement begin?"

"Well, I first became acquainted with it through four visitors from the United States," Kerr said. "They were from Redeemer Episcopal Church in Houston, Texas."

I was familiar with Redeemer Church. It had been featured on the CBS television network because of its involvement in the charismatic movement. In 1971, its minister, Graham Pulkingham, and members of his staff visited Belfast. They made quite an impression on a lot of people. But Kerr was cautious.

Months later he visited the Institute of Religion and Human Development in the United States. It gave him an opportunity to attend the special services at Redeemer Church in Houston. Kerr was amazed at what he saw. He returned to Belfast anxious to see such a renewal on his campus.

"It is an interesting thing," he said. "Not long ago, we watched the videotape of Billy Graham's lecture. He said something that I didn't notice the first time. He said that if a revival could begin in the university, it would spread across the country."

Kerr arranged a room for me adjacent to his office. There I spent a long afternoon interviewing students. Some of their stories were fantastic. They spoke of visions and the mysterious gifts of the Holy Spirit, but all of the interviews included one recurring trend. "Something in life was missing," they would say. Then they would explain the Jesus experience.

Richard Harper was a handsome, young scientist. At eighteen he was sworn into the Orange Order in a secret ceremony in Crumlin. It seemed unusual for Richard, an Orangeman, to be rubbing shoulders with Catholics and students like Patrick Murphy, the young socialist. But such was the ecumenicity of this prayer group.

Richard was in his second year of research for his Ph.D. in chemistry. At first his goals were purely academic. He wanted to be a scientist. But the novelty of science wore off as he began to realize its limitations.

"I had friends who were Christians at the time. I knew that they had something in their lives that I didn't."

"What do you mean?" I asked. "Everyone I interview here says the same thing. What made them different?"

"Well, they were friendly. They would invite me to their parties and to the beach." Richard hesitated. "I don't know. I can't explain it."

One night in 1968 Richard's friends invited him to a Billy Graham rally. The rally was taking place in London but could be seen by closed-circuit relay in the Ulster Hall in Belfast. Richard had a date with one of the Church of Ireland girls.

"Billy Graham didn't say anything I hadn't heard before, but it just clicked. I realized that though I had been attending the Church of Ireland for years, I had never really become a Christian intellectually, or on the inside. I had to go down to the front. I was very emotionally upset. I didn't want to look foolish to Jill. I felt that God was real, but even spiritual things I approached from a scientific point of view."

Richard responded to the American evangelist's appeal to walk to the front for counseling. He was greeted by a member of the Church of Ireland who read a verse from the Bible, John 3:16.

"What about the first chapter of Genesis?" Richard asked immediately.

The man couldn't answer him. He ignored the question and continued on with the same game plan by reading the next verse he was supposed to read.

"The universe must be very old," Richard said. "The Andromeda Nebula is two million light-years away, so it must be at least that old."

Now the man asked Richard to sign a card committing his life to Christ.

"I can't," Richard answered. "I have too many questions yet." It seemed so childish and foolish to him.

The following year during the pressures of final exams, he dropped out of church altogether. He left his spiritual decisions unresolved. There were just too many more important things to do.

During the Christmas vacation of 1969, he was in bed with the flu. He was hoping to rest and then return to his studies. But the illness lingered for weeks, leaving him drained.

He returned to Queen's University and found it impossible to catch up. He studied long hours into the night. It seemed that he had even forgotten some of the things he had previously learned.

Mentally exhausted and physically weak, Richard seemed to be nearing a breaking point. At times he imagined an ominous evil influence or spirit around him. His personality would change. He tried to maintain his scientific rationale.

On one occasion he discovered he could read people's thoughts. He frightened a room full of university students by demonstrating his power. Richard himself was left shaken by the experience. A Christian friend explained to him that it was a spiritual problem. "There may even be a demonic or evil spiritual influence using you."

That's when Richard Harper was persuaded to contact a charismatic minister, Keith Gerner. Keith prayed over him. Richard describes it as a prayer of deliverance.

One night Richard awakened in his room at Queen's. There was no grogginess. He was instantly and completely awake in one moment. He was in hysterics, and his body was covered with sweat.

"I'm going to die," he thought. "I must be going out of mind. But I know I'm going to die." He was very scared, but within ten minutes he managed to calm himself down.

Richard Harper began to pray. He prayed for a miracle. He had never believed in miracles. He had never believed that Jesus had healed the sick. He had never believed that Jesus had turned the water to wine. As a chemist, he knew it was just impossible. But now he needed God. He needed the God he had felt at the Billy Graham rally.

The room was suddenly warm. Richard looked up. It was as though Jesus had come into the room.

"I was overwhelmed by the fact that God loved me. It was all so real. Nobody had to tell me God existed—I knew. There was a peace I could feel."

I shifted in my seat. "How long did that peace last?" I asked.

"It has never stopped," he smiled.

"How can you, as an Orangeman, work together with these Catholic prayer groups?"

"Well, that is a miracle of the Holy Spirit. I love the Catholics as much as anyone else. I visited a convent in

Hollywood, just ten miles south of here. The sisters were so kind, and I could see the love of God on their faces."

Neither one of us said anything for a moment. Richard shrugged his shoulders as if to say, *I don't know what else I could tell you about what has been happening to me.*

Then, as I turned off my tape recorder he said, "I don't know if I should say this," he hesitated, "but in all fairness, I still don't understand the first chapter of Genesis."

We both laughed.

"Have you read *Genesis in Space and Time?"* I asked.

"Who is the author?"

"Francis Schaeffer."

He closed his eyes as though he was concentrating on something important that he wanted to express. "I don't need to know everything now. At times science has been a great disappointment to me."

Richard Harper stood and our interview ended.

Perhaps the most fascinating personality of the day was Patricia Moore. She was a third-year French major at Queen's. She wore huge, dark-rimmed glasses and talked with a pleasant, soft voice.

"It seemed as though I had come to an end to myself. I was frustrated. I prayed about it. Then one day I was walking on the footpath out there." She glanced out onto the campus. "I met these two men from Houston, Texas. They were talking with some students."

"Graham Pulkingham of Redeemer Church?" I asked.

"Yes, I believe so, and there was a doctor with them."

"Go on—sorry for interrupting."

"Well, I stopped and listened. They were talking about renewal, and I realized as they were speaking that this was what I had been searching for."

"How did you know that?" I asked curiously.

"I can't explain it," she answered.

A loud truck roared slowly up the street and momentarily drowned out our conversation.

"There was a meeting that night," Patricia continued. "I didn't even know about it."

"Was it here at the center?"

"No. It was at the church. The people from Houston were speaking. There were only fifteen or twenty students there. I came late. It was eleven o'clock at night."

"What happened?"

"Well, it was almost over, but you could feel this holy feeling, like—the Spirit of God. Then they had us come to the front of the church and they prayed over us. They prayed that we might speak in tongues as a sign that we had received the baptism of the Holy Spirit."

"Did you speak in tongues?" I smiled.

"You know," Patricia looked out of the window again. "I had never heard of this speaking-in-tongues business. Some of the other students prayed that way, but I didn't want to. I just committed my life to God and asked Jesus to take complete control."

"Were you in a trance or something?"

"Oh, no. Nothing like that. It was a happy thing, really. It was strange because I had never had peace like that. But I did speak in tongues."

"Oh, you did?"

"Yes. I went back to my seat near the door, but I didn't want to leave the peaceful atmosphere. So I just knelt down and prayed again where I was. Suddenly my praises just didn't seem enough, and this other language came out."

"Was it an emotional experience?"

Patricia smiled this time. "No, it was a very natural thing. I felt so close to God. It was very much between me and God."

"Have you felt this close to God since that moment?"

"Yes. There are times when I feel like praying to Him. There is so much trouble here, you know. I will pray in tongues, and there is this joy, or new peace. I don't know what to make of it." She shook her hair gently back on her shoulders. "I was alone last summer. I wasn't included in the group over in Europe on the continent. But you know, I didn't feel alone at all because I really felt that God was with me during that time."

I thanked Patricia for her interview. "This movement is really spreading," I commented.

"Yes, and you know that's strange. I was in France a year

and a half ago. God gave me a vision"—she was apologetic—"I guess you would call it that, I don't know. Anyway, I saw a group of people, Catholics and Protestants. They were holding hands and singing together. Then I came home to all this bombing. There was trouble crossing the border, so I wondered if God had given me the dream or not."

I glanced outside. Somehow the day was coming to an end even though it had just begun. "How do you interpret your dream now?" I asked, packing my tape recorder and gathering my notes.

"Oh, it's come true," she said radiantly. "At the conference in Benburb on the border. The charismatic prayer groups came together, Protestant and Catholic. It was wonderful."

The taxi ride back to the Europa Hotel was much quicker this time. *I want to interview some of the Catholics now,* I thought to myself. *And then maybe I should visit Benburb.*

I stared dreamily out the window at a row of demolished buildings. Occasionally I strained to read the graffiti scrawled on the brick walls. "UP the IRA," one said.

When we turned onto Great Victoria Street, I saw the Donaldson and Lyttle's furniture store. It had been leveled.

"Let me out here," I called to the driver.

There wasn't much sunlight left, but I clicked some pictures. The air was cold but invigorating. After those long hours in a stuffy room interviewing students, it felt good to get outside.

The charismatic movement and the afternoon with the students seemed far away to me then. I stared down at the rubble. *There's still a war going on,* I thought. *For eight centuries they have been fighting each other. It will take more than the charismatic renewal to bring peace to Ulster.*

When I turned, I stared straight across the street. It was just as though God was saying something. On a large board hanging from the Great Victoria Street Baptist Church was a poster, "Salvation is of the Lord. Call unto Me and I will answer thee, and show thee great and mighty things that thou knowest not."

# 12

# After Bloody Sunday

January 30, 1972, will long be remembered in modern Irish history as Bloody Sunday, when soldiers of the British parachute regiment lowered their rifles into a crowd of marching Catholics and fired. Thousands of unarmed civilians ran screaming in horror. Most of those who died were shot in the back.

The civil rights movement had announced a march and a rally in Londonderry. Bernadette Devlin was one of the speakers; thousands were expected to attend. The government declared the march illegal and brought in British troops to break it up.

The soldiers were nervous; they were in enemy territory. They were also frustrated; forty-eight had died in sniper attacks and the British military had still not determined how to contain the IRA.

No one knows who fired the first shot. A British investigation led by England's Chief Justice Lord Widgery claimed that someone from the crowd fired on the soldiers first, but none of the dead or wounded Catholics were armed. The soldiers opened fire. The crowd hit the ground. For twenty minutes the soldiers shot at anything that moved.

At the Rosemount Roman Catholic convent in Dublin that evening, the sisters had not yet heard of the Londonderry massacre. Sister Elizabeth sat in the lounge waiting for the news to come on television. The news is always a favorite at the convent.

From the opening reports the sisters knew that something terrible had happened in the North. A roomful of quiet nuns watched in bewilderment as the story unfolded.

Wives and mothers cried into the cameras, "Oh, God, they've gone crazy! They're shooting everybody! Oh, God!" A man waved a white handkerchief at the soldiers and rushed out into the street to a dying boy, only to be shot in the head himself.

"Stop it! Stop it!" a hysterical young teen-age girl shouted at the soldiers, looking up from her dying brother.

Even the news commentators were stunned. There was not much discussion, just the report.

It was awkward in the Rosemount convent; some of the sisters were English. But even they were appalled.

Sister Elizabeth had an immediate response. "That's typical of the British troops. They never give a damn about the people. It's just the Catholic minority they oppress!"

Her revolutionary sympathies surfaced. "The British are so imperialistic," she said.

Sister Elizabeth was a leader in the charismatic renewal in Dublin, a very ecumenical movement indeed, but at that moment she sympathized with the IRA or anyone who would stand up against such violence.

Elizabeth Keane had come from a traditional Irish background. She was the youngest of nine children. The family lived in Dublin. All of her brothers and sisters were involved in politics. They were very republican and nationalistic. They were also good Catholics; two of her brothers are now priests.

"I never questioned my belief or faith," she says.

Elizabeth was greatly influenced by the life of Tom Dooley, the medical missionary. She loved people. She joined a religious congregation, the Medical Missionaries of Mary.

Sister Elizabeth made great friends at the University College in Dublin. "Yet something was funny," she says. "Though we were Christians, Christ was never mentioned. At the end of the year, it began to disturb some of us."

Elizabeth joined two other young men in an attempt to start a new socialist group. The idea was to bring Christianity into some of the political debates. But the group never got off the ground. "We could never agree on anything. We couldn't even define 'the social group.' "

During the summer of 1971, some of the sisters in the convent began to read about the Pentecostal movement. They were all impressed by the testimonies of joy and especially how Jesus Christ seemed so real to Pentecostals. But the charismatic movement seemed so far away from Dublin.

One afternoon Sister Marion received a letter from Taiwan. She passed Elizabeth in the cloakroom of the convent. "Listen, do you really want to read something?" Marion asked.

Elizabeth read the letter from Madeliene deBlanc, a mother superior of a house in Formosa. She said that she needed a renewal. She told how some people prayed for her and how she had allowed the Holy Spirit to come into her life. She told how her life had been dead and empty, and how it was now absolutely transformed.

"It sounds banal to talk about joy, and love, and peace, and hope," Sister Elizabeth said, "but you could see that these things were real to her."

A few days later Elizabeth met with her two friends to discuss their socialist program for the coming year. They were talking together while eating their lunch in the restaurant at the university.

"You know, I have been reading about the Pentecostal movement," Elizabeth said. "Maybe that is for us."

"No!" Ray Reynolds answered immediately. "Pentecostalism is out. We are not going to mention it."

"Okay." Elizabeth didn't care.

But, several weeks later the three attended a meeting of the Student Christian Movement (SCM) at White Abbey. A Presbyterian minister named Smaile and a Catholic priest spoke on the charismatic renewal. The Presbyterian was especially enthusiastic.

"Excuse me," one of Elizabeth's friends asked, "but do you always live and speak at this fever pitch?"

Only days later Madeliene deBlanc, the mother superior from Formosa, was passing through Dublin, planning to meet a Chinese priest. When Elizabeth heard the news, she was excited. She began to wonder whether God was gently leading her into this charismatic movement. One of the young men invited Sister Madeliene to meet them. A meeting was arranged at the Kimmage Manor, house of the Holy Ghost fathers.

On December 9, 1971, they met together. The Chinese priest and Sister Madeliene each explained what happened to them and how the charismatic movement was spreading in Asia.

Elizabeth Keane listened carefully. "This is it. I have been praying and waiting for this for a long time." But she was worried. *Tomorrow they'll be leaving,* she thought.

Madeliene was spending the night at the convent. On the way home, Elizabeth asked for prayer. She told Marion, "If I don't have it now, I'll never have it."

That night Sister Marion and Sister Madeliene led Elizabeth into the tiny kitchen for a prayer of renewal. Elizabeth knelt as the other sisters surrounded her and laid hands on her shoulders.

"In faith I asked the Lord to change my life in whatever way He wanted to."

Elizabeth left the other two sisters and went up to the chapel. She opened her Bible and glanced down at a verse, "Everything you ask in prayer, believing, you shall receive."

From that moment on, peace, joy, and hope began to build in her life. "It really did completely change me," Elizabeth says. "Jesus came into my life as a real person."

But she was afraid to tell her socialist friends.

Seven weeks later Sister Elizabeth sat in the lounge of the Rosemount convent listening to the news of the 'Derry massacre. Thirteen young Catholics died; many were wounded. The college was in an uproar. "There's going to be a march tomorrow," someone said. Elizabeth decided to join them.

Thousands of students began the march from University College to the British embassy. For five miles the students were silent, but there was tremendous emotion. Anger built with each step. Elizabeth was afraid something would go wrong.

When they finally spilled into the square, there were tens of thousands. They were screaming now. Elizabeth was appalled by the fierce anger, and she worried as she felt herself being taken in by the mob emotion.

The police made a couple of baton charges, but it was useless. Molotov cocktails smashed through the windows of the British embassy. Soon it was ablaze.

Sister Elizabeth was terribly confused. She knew intuitively that it was wrong to be a part of the mob emotion. She worked her way out of the square to a side street. There she lingered for a moment. Tall flames licked the brick shell of the large building. The glow of the great fire reflected off her face. Here were thousands of people momentarily sympathizing and united behind the political position she had worked for all her life. *I know it's wrong,* she thought, *but it's still good to see the British embassy burn.*

Tuesday, a special ecumenical memorial service was held for those who had died in 'Derry. Elizabeth and her young socialist friends attended. "I was sitting in the audience listening to the ministers. They were all saying nice things, but all I could feel was that they were handing out only platitudes."

The students in the audience—the few who bothered to attend—were indifferent. They had already gotten rid of their emotion.

Then someone representing the maintenance workers at the college stood up. He was not articulate, but everyone was struck by what he said. "The only thing that keeps coming back to me is that God said we must love one another. I don't understand it, but God said it. Somewhere we have got to love one another."

The words hit Elizabeth like a dagger. For a moment she felt ashamed. She remembered the night in the convent when she had experienced the love of Christ through Sister Madeliene. Elizabeth left the memorial service determined that love would predominate over everything.

Charismatic prayer meetings began at Kimmage Manor. Soon Elizabeth's socialist friends were leaders in the group. News of what was happening spread through Dublin. They wanted to limit the attendance until they knew where they were going. That was impossible. Within a few weeks sixty were visiting the special meetings.

Then one day Elizabeth heard some amazing news. The charismatic renewal had begun in Belfast. There was a small group, only eight or nine, but it was a beginning.

"Maybe someday we can get together," she thought. "Maybe the Holy Spirit can unite the Irish."

One year after Bloody Sunday, Sister Elizabeth saw it happen. Catholics and Protestants, Orangemen and republicans met together at Benburb.

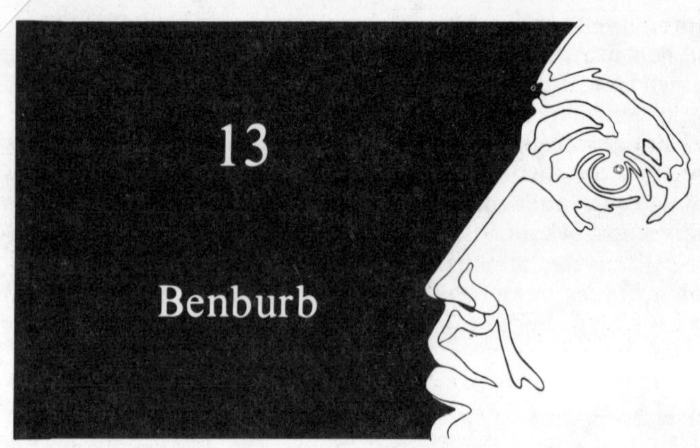

# 13

# Benburb

Rev. Cecil Kerr, chaplain of Queen's University, had called the conference and had personally suggested the Servite Monastery in Benburb as a good location. Only the previous year he had objected when the chaplains at Queen's had wanted to have a freshman retreat in Benburb. Now, deeply involved in the charismatic movement, he was quite willing to go to the Catholic center.

Benburb is a beautiful, idyllic, little village near the border that separates the two Irelands. It is reminiscent of more pleasant moments in Irish history. Only a hundred yards from the monastery are the ruins of a sixteenth-century castle. There are rocks and mountains, tennis courts, and a garden.

But the beauty of the area is deceptive. Only weeks before, three British soldiers had been ambushed by the IRA near Benburb. They were blown up in their Salacen vehicles and scraped off the road. Days later, the IRA visited the Benburb itself. They ran down the mountain slope, crossed the river, and climbed over the walls of the little village, firing warning shots into the air. The local telephone exchange was bombed, damaging the nearby Anglican church.

One week later, Catholics and Protestants united for the January 1973 charismatic conference.

As the delegates nervously registered, Patricia Moore

noticed an older nun. Her vision of a large group of Catholics and Protestants uniting with their arms around each other still seemed unrealistic. The old nun lived in an entirely different world. Patricia closely studied the many wrinkles in her face and noticed the sister's habit. She had never really looked closely at the garb of a Catholic nun. It seemed so medieval. Though she could actually have reached out and touched the old woman, it seemed they were miles apart.

Not everyone at the conference was so apprehensive. To Robin Lee, a young Church of Ireland delegate from Belfast, the conference was already historic. Robin was helping register the many delegates when a chartered bus from Dublin pulled up. Among the many who stepped off the bus was Jim Finn, a young Catholic. Robin had met Jim two years before in England. Their reunion at Benburb was something of a miracle.

The two young men were speechless. Then they burst into laughter.

Robin thought back to the summer of 1971 when he first met Jim in England. During the summer the English import cheap Irish labor. The two Irishmen found themselves living in the same boardinghouse and working next to each other in a factory.

There was one big problem. Jim Finn was a republican studying to be a Catholic priest. Robin Lee was an Ulsterman planning to be a Church of Ireland minister. Their ideas clashed immediately.

Finally, they decided that the only way to live together would be to talk only about things they had in common. The two often took long walks at night to escape the stuffy boardinghouse. Robin felt free to share his most intimate goals and dreams.

"Some nights we talked about home," Robin said. "If my folks knew I was spending most of my time with a Catholic, they would have been very upset."

One night just before they returned to Ireland, they began to talk about Christ and what it meant to be a Christian. It was late in the summer, and they knew that the long walks in the English countryside were coming to an end.

"Christ is really walking beside us right now," Jim Finn said.

Robin took a deep breath of air. "Won't it be wonderful when He returns?" he commented, looking out into the universe. "When that happens, we can come together and show the rest of the people in Ireland that we are really brothers."

Both of them concluded it would probably never happen.

In the following two years, each in his own way had experienced Christ, and both had been swept into the charismatic movement. Now they met in Benburb as brothers.

At the very first session, the delegates began to sense that something special was happening. Rev. Cecil Kerr opened the meeting by inviting people to stand and share or speak about Christianity.

The very first one was a young man from the Shankill Road. The Shankill Road is perhaps the most famous militant Protestant area of Belfast. The Protestant Shankill Road and the Catholic Falls Road are separated by a barbed wire barrier referred to in Ulster as the "Berlin Wall."

The young man explained how he had been baptized in the Holy Spirit and how his life was now overflowing with love.

Immediately, across the room a Catholic woman stood. She explained that she was a teacher in Andersonstown, a Catholic IRA stronghold in Belfast. "I asked God to let me meet someone from the Shankill Road," she said excitedly. "I just wanted to share something of the love of Christ which has come into my life."

The atmosphere in the room began to grow warm as she explained how God had changed her life. "I was very active in the Catholic civil rights movement, but one night after a rally in Armagh, I realized that many of us were manifesting a real class hatred. I felt this could not be right. That night when I went home I felt God speaking to me, and my life was changed."

As each person stood to share his own story, a feeling of unity and love seemed to sweep across the monastery grounds.

On Saturday afternoon Mr. and Mrs. Larry Kelly of Belfast arrived. Larry had been introduced to the charismatic movement by Frank Forte, the Catholic who founded the first prayer group in Northern Ireland. Larry, a Catholic himself, eventually started his own prayer group, which involved Catholics and Protestants. By now his prayer group was the most truly ecumenical in all of Ireland. Yet, Mr. Kelly was nervous.

"By nature, I am a very cautious person," he told me. "I wasn't planning on going."

But his wife felt that the weekend would be a nice escape from Belfast and their children. It turned out to be, in Larry's words "an event of major significance for Ireland."

Saturday evening the delegates assembled in the crypt chapel beneath the monastery. There the Irish Catholics and Protestants united for the Holy Eucharist. As far as anyone knows, it was the first time in Ireland's long history that such an event took place. Later, there was criticism from both Catholics and Protestants; at subsequent conferences the spirit of unity has continued, but there has not been another united communion.

"It is in the Eucharist that we cannot be united," Rev. Cecil Kerr explains. "By having intercommunion we would be inviting criticism from people who don't understand. I think we would be jeopardizing the movement."

Frank Forte agrees, "We have to recognize our differences and learn to respect each other."

But the event of the first Benburb conference called for a special kind of celebration.

The crypt chapel was very small. The delegates crowded into the room, most of them seated on the floor.

Bill and Francis Tanner, Catholics from Belfast, were quite surprised to find that non-Catholics were going to receive the Mass too. Larry Kelly was equally concerned. When he entered the crypt chapel, they were singing songs together. Having previously taken the Mass that day, he could not take it again, so he was able to glance around the room and watch the proceedings.

As the singing continued, a mysterious group emotion began to envelop the delegates. An almost electrical surge of joy began to jump from one person to the next.

A modern mural of Our Lady looked down from the wall. There was a brief moment of silence, and then everyone broke into singing.

We are one in the Spirit.
We are one in the Lord.
And we pray that all unity
May one day be restored.
And they'll know we are Christians
By our love, by our love.
Yes, they'll know we are Christians
By our love.

Larry Kelly saw Sister Elizabeth sitting on the floor in the center of the room. "There was such joy on her face," he says, "and I have never sensed such a spirit of unity."

It didn't seem to make any difference who was Catholic or Protestant. Some of the students put their arms around each other. Frank Forte says, "It was tremendous. There was a bond of love."

Pat Murphy was there. He thought back to a labor rally in Belfast where they had passed out fifteen thousand leaflets calling for Catholics and Protestants to come together. There had not been one response.

"I finally realized that we as socialists could not change the situation in Ireland. Neither can the British with all of their tanks and all of their guns. Only the Spirit of God can save us."

Patricia Moore found herself seated next to the old Catholic nun whom she had noticed in the registration line. "It was really wonderful," Patricia says, "because then I knew that there were really no barriers between us at all. We were praising God and we were really one."

The priest began the communion service. After distributing the pieces of bread a quiet reverence descended. The whole ceremony was suspended in midair. Pat Murphy sat smiling dreamily into the ceiling. One of the priests closed his eyes tightly.

Then suddenly some of the students began to sing softly in prayer languages. Other counter-melodies came from other parts of the room, and soon the whole chapel was filled with voices singing to God in unknown languages of praise. Ingeniously the various melodies harmonized with a sound that was in itself a miracle. Then as mysteriously as it had all started, it suddenly stopped.

Early Sunday morning, the first rays of sunlight spread across the Irish countryside. Sally Brown yawned and stretched as the old clock in the village, which had interrupted her sleep twice, gonged six times. Like many of the delegates, she was planning to attend the special services at the local Anglican church. Rev. Cecil Kerr had been invited to speak. Sally, an Anglican herself, was curious how he would handle the situation.

Benburb's Protestants were upset by the activities at the Catholic monastery. Most of them had not heard about the charismatic movement, and they could not understand what the Catholics and Protestants were doing together. Only the week before, their tiny cathedral had been damaged by IRA bombing. Some believed that the Catholics of Benburb were harboring IRA terrorists. Suspicions ran so deep that the local Anglican priest would not enter the monastery.

That Sunday morning the crowd seemed larger than usual. The organist nervously touched the wrong key. The old organ magnified the mistake a hundred times, sending an inharmonious chord out to the audience. The organist didn't correct it, either. She stubbornly held the chord to the very end of the measure, glaring out to the audience as though it were their mistake.

Chaplain Kerr sat quietly glancing up to the stained-glass windows, some of which had been destroyed by the previous week of bombing. He remembered his own prejudice. He had carefully rehearsed his sermon, but at that moment he wondered if his comments would be very effective.

Then he began to consciously focus on what his eyes had been staring at. High at the top of the sanctuary were three windows. On each was portrayed one of the three Christian virtues: faith, hope, and love. Only something was missing. He stared for a moment and then realized what was wrong. The window with hope was not there. It had evidently been blown out by the IRA bomb and now was replaced by plain glass.

"We have lost all hope," Kerr told his audience in conclusion that morning. He pointed dramatically to the windows. "Hope has been blown to pieces by the bombs and the violence. But we still have love. God has given us that love, and no terrorist or sniper or even the demons of hell can ever take it away from us. And we still have faith. Faith to believe that this love God has allowed us to experience here in Benburb on a small scale may some day sweep across all of Ireland."

Those words were prophetic. Before the year ended, the movement spread from Dublin and Belfast to Limerick, Newry, Kildare, Enis, Cork, Coleraine, Bangor, Armagh, and more than twenty other Irish cities. The renewal movement began at Saint Patrick's College in Maynooth, and the Irish neo-Pentecostals began publishing their own magazine.

By Monday evening, most of the charismatic delegates had returned home. Robin Lee had planned to stay an extra day. By coincidence, Jim Finn had made similiar plans.

That night they took a long walk together through the monastery grounds. A cold wind rustled through the trees, but the moon was big and bright and seemed to welcome their company. For more than twenty minutes neither one of them said one word.

They thought back to their summer in England. They remembered their long walks together through the countryside. They remembered what they had said about Catholics and Protestants living together in peace. They were still surprised by the mysterious way that fate had brought them back together again. Both of them were overwhelmed by the events of the past weekend.

Jim Finn sat down on a large rock. The moon reflected in a thousand different places in the river below him. "Well," he said, as though to pick up their conversation where they had left off two years before, "it is happening."

Robin Lee stared out into the sky at the stars, the same stars that had watched eight centuries of hatred and war in Ireland . . . and he wondered, *Is it really happening?*

# Epilogue

Paris was warm. The sun was setting. Soon the monuments would be lit up by spotlights, the fountains would spray, and the whole city would come to life. I sat alone on a bench in the Tuileries gardens watching two lovers stroll around a shallow reflecting pool.

*Wow, it's good to get out of Northern Ireland,* I thought. *It's so peaceful here.* There was a constant pressure and terror in Northern Ireland that I didn't fully understand until I got out.

The Eiffel Tower peaked above the trees. To my right I looked down on the Place de la Concorde, where the cars circled round and round. An ancient Egyptian obelisk stood proudly in the center of the square, a souvenir of one of Napoleon's great battles. It was relaxing just to sit outside in the evening air without having to worry about bombs or snipers.

I thought I could hear the voice of my wife, Gloria, coming from the trees. I turned around to see her. She smiled, her long blonde hair blowing slightly in the breeze.

"I've got the food." She held up a sack.

We spread our food out on a newspaper. There was cheese, salami, a wide variety of fruit, and several long rolls of bread.

"Oh, honey, I didn't tell you," Gloria said excitedly, continuing where she had left off at the hotel. "While you were in Ulster I saw Deborah Kerr in some play in London. I can't remember the name of it, but I have the program in our room."

"Deborah Kerr?" I asked.

"Yes, Deborah Kerr," she replied. "Only I was so tired from the flight over the Atlantic that I fell asleep." We both laughed.

After our snack together, we strolled down the magnificent avenue, Champs-Elysées, passing theaters and sidewalk cafes. Every once in a while we glanced up at the great Arc de Triomphe, which grew larger with every step.

A crowd of American tourists came pushing out of a night club. They were angry and a little drunk.

"What a gyp!" one old man said disgustedly.

His wife was a little disillusioned herself. "Maybe the night show is better," she said.

We smiled. *Life really is empty at times,* I thought. Gloria and I had traveled all over the world. We had seen the diamond mines of South Africa, the sparkling Hong Kong Bay, the magnificent mountain peaks of New Zealand, and the deserts of Australia. We had toured the great cities of Europe and shopped on the fabulous Ginza in Tokyo. Yes, people are all the same; everyone is looking for satisfaction and peace. Yet, peace is so elusive and so hard to find.

"Remember that Greek restaurant in the Latin Quarter?" Gloria asked. "You said we could go there this time."

"Are you hungry already?" I laughed.

"Well, I didn't eat that much," she pouted.

"How do you keep such a good figure and still eat so much?"

She grabbed my hand. "Here's a Metro entrance," she said, and we darted down the stairs to the subway.

Minutes later we were sitting in a dimly lit Greek restaurant packed with students and tourists.

Gloria was talking about her shopping bargains in London. My thoughts were far away. I was thinking about Ireland and all the trouble. I remembered a story my father once told me.

There was a special art contest, and each of the artists were asked to paint a picture depicting peace. Among the many entrees were beautiful scenes of mountains, lakes, meadows, and lots of clouds. But the picture which won the prize was a scene of a violent storm. At the very bottom of the canvas was a dove protected by huge rocks. The bird was resting very peacefully, right in the midst of the storm.

My father is a very religious man. He said that if people really have faith in God, they will be at their best in times of trouble.

I thought about Northern Ireland and the terrible war. For the first time I began to feel good about it. Some of the people I had met in Ireland had real peace. They had faith in God in spite of all the trouble around them.

Gloria suddenly interrupted my thoughts. "You said hardly a word about what happened in Ireland." She had to shout above the din of noise.

"You won't believe it when I tell you," I teased her.

"Come on, now, tell me," she answered. I laughed.

Our bearded waiter arrived with long skewers of shish kebob.

I felt good all of a sudden. I grabbed Gloria's hand. "It will take all night for me to tell you."

"I don't care," she smiled. "Tell me everything that happened from the first moment you arrived."

I pushed a piece of tender steak off the skewer and onto my wooden plate. "Well, it all began with a visit to Duggan's Tavern."